Jim Britt's

Cracking the Rich Code¹²

Inspiring Stories, Insights and Strategies from Top Thought Leaders Around the World

STAY IN TOUCH WITH JIM BRITT

www.JimBritt.com

www.JimBrittVentures.com

www.JimBrittCoaching.com

www.CrackingTheRichCode.com

www.becomeAcoauthor.com

Cracking the Rich Code[12]

Jim Britt

All Rights Reserved

Copyright 2024

CTRC Publishing and Training, Inc.

10556 Combie Road, Suite 6205

Auburn, CA 95602

The use of any part of this publication, whether reproduced, stored in any retrieval system, or transmitted in any forms or by any means, electronic or otherwise, without the prior written consent of the publisher, is an infringement of copyright law.

Jim Britt

Cracking the Rich Code[12]

SHU# 2370000894288

Co-authors from Around the World

Jim Britt

Yarona Boster

Katie Augustine

Suzanne Sullivan

James & Rebecca Lockwood

Smita Das Jain

David Radosevich

Victor Bullara II

Baz Porter

Julie Hruska

Elke Philips

Andrew Franseen

Karen Justice

Kim Malloy

Deborah Kaler

Adriana Gattermayr

Dr, Susy Francis Best

Alba Contreras Rodriguez

Raymond Michael Rivera

Raeanne Lacatena

Mary Hunter

DEDICATION

Entrepreneurs will change the world. They always have and they always will.

Dedicated to the entrepreneurial spirit that lives within each of us.

God Bless America and the World!

PREFACE

Jim Britt

The worlds top 50 most influential speakers and top 20 life and success strategist.

In pursuit of a meaningful and fulfilling life, the concept of richness extends far beyond mere financial prosperity. It encompasses a holistic approach, embracing abundance in every facet of our existence—financial, emotional, intellectual, and spiritual. "Cracking the Rich Code with 21 Top Thought Leaders" is not just a manual for accumulating wealth; it is a comprehensive guide to attaining riches in all areas of life.

The journey to holistic riches is a transformative odyssey, and within these pages, you'll find the collective wisdom of 21 experts who have not only achieved remarkable success in their respective field but, have also cracked the code to living a truly rich and fulfilling life, while helping other to do the same. Their stories, insights, and strategies are the keys to unlocking doors to prosperity abundance and well-being.

Our esteemed contributors are visionaries who understand that true richness transcends financial accomplishments. Their perspectives span the spectrum, from business, to personal development, mindfulness, relationships, health and wellness, and spirituality. Each chapter in this book serves as a beacon of guidance, offering a unique perspective on how to navigate the intricate pathways of life to attain richness in all dimensions.

As you delve into the following pages, you'll be introduced to the stories of these remarkable individuals who have not only achieved success in their respective fields, but have also cultivated richness in their relationships, health, and sense of purpose. Their experiences are a testament to the idea that true wealth is a compellation of material prosperity and the riches found in our connections, personal growth, and the alignment of our actions with our deepest values.

True richness moves beyond the material realm into emotional richness. Emotional intelligence, resilience, and the ability to navigate the complexities of human relationships. Each coauthor offers practical tools and perspectives that will empower you to forge deeper connections, overcome challenges, and find joy in your everyday interactions.

Intellectual richness is also a dimension often overlooked in the pursuit of a rich life. From innovation and creativity to conscious learning and adaptability, intellectual richness is the fuel that propels us forward. All creation begins with an idea. The contributors share their insights into cultivating a curious mind, staying ahead of a rapidly changing world, and leveraging knowledge to create a life of richness and purpose.

Spiritual richness takes center stage too. Beyond religious affiliations, spiritual richness encompasses a profound connection with oneself, others, and the universe. These thought leaders share their journeys of self-discovery, mindfulness, and the pursuit of a higher purpose, offering a more rich and meaningful existence.

This book is not a one-size-fits-all prescription for richness; it a diverse tapestry of ideas, experiences, and strategies that you can tailor to your unique journey. Whether you are an entrepreneur seeking business and financial success, or an individual navigating the complexities of relationships. A lifelong learner, or someone on a spiritual quest, "Cracking the Rich Code" has something for you.

As you embark on this transformative journey with our diverse lineup of thought leaders and experts, just remember that richness is not a destination but a continuous exploration. May the insights and strategies within these pages serve as catalysts for your personal and collective growth, guiding you toward a life of richness in every sense of the word.

Wishing you abundance fulfillment, and richness in all areas of your life.

And remember, just one idea acted upon can change your life. Happy hunting!

Jim Britt

www.JimBritt.com

www.CrackingTheRichCode.com

Foreword by Brian Tracy

Life is always a series of transitions… people, places and things that shape who we are as individuals. Often, you never know that the next catalyst for change is just around the corner, in someone you meet, on a page of a book or in a moment of self-reflection.

As the author of 93 books myself, you can imagine how fussy I am to write a foreword to publications in the business and self-development space. My friend Jim Britt is an exception. He has spent decades influencing millions of individuals with his many best-selling books, seminars, programs and coaching, to blossom into the best version of themselves. He has the knowledge, wisdom and skillsets needed to make a significant contribution to overcoming issues entrepreneurs face in business today. His success speaks for itself.

In a world where the pursuit of wealth and success often dominates our collective consciousness, the concept of cracking the rich code has become an elusive quest for many. We marvel at the seemingly effortless success stories of millionaires and billionaires, wondering what secret knowledge or hidden talents they possess that have propelled them to riches. Yet, behind every success story lies a unique and inspiring journey, woven with challenges, triumphs, and invaluable lessons learned.

It is with great excitement that I present to you "Cracking the Rich Code," a book that unveils the remarkable successes of 20 millionaire coauthors. These individuals have not only achieved extraordinary success, but have also generously shared their insights, strategies, and wisdom, inviting the readers to embark on their own transformative journeys.

Within these pages you will discover a variety of stories that defy the myth of an easily attainable overnight success. Instead, you will discover stories of resilience, determination and the unrelenting decisions to pursue their dreams. Each author offers a unique perspective on wealth creation, sharing the secrets they unlocked along their path to financial success.

As you read each chapter you will encounter diverse backgrounds, highlighting the fact that the rich code is not for a certain gender, race, age or social status. You will discover that there are a myriad of ways in which financial success can be achieved.

So, prepare to be inspired as you witness the transformative power of perseverance and the unwavering belief in one's abilities. Through their stories, each coauthor will take you behind the scenes of their successes, allowing you a glimpse into the countless hours of hard work, sacrifices, and failures they encountered along the way.

This book is not just about destination; it's about the journey. Beyond the accumulation of wealth, these authors emphasize the importance of personal growth, finding purpose, and making a positive impact on the world. They share their experience of self-discovery and self-improvement, and offer guidance on developing the mindset, habits, and values necessary to build sustainable success in any and all areas of life.

Their stories will reveal that the rich code is not a hidden secret, but rather a blueprint for anyone willing to embrace the principles with dedication and perseverance. It's about learning from failures, embracing risks, overcoming fears, and continuously expanding one's knowledge and skills. It's about having a mindset of abundance, nurturing relationships, and giving back to society.

Whether you are an aspiring entrepreneur, a seasoned professional, or simply seeking inspiration and guidance, "Cracking the Rich Code" will provide a roadmap to unlocking your real potential. Through the diverse perspectives of Jim Britt and the coauthors, you will find a wealth of actionable strategies, that will empower you to rewrite your own story and chart your course toward financial prosperity.

Let's help in this quest, as Jim Britt and the talented coauthors unselfishly donate their most important asset, their precious LIFETIME of experience, to elevate one life at a time to their full potential and greatness.

If I were you, I would buy 10, and then giftwrap them to acknowledge your most important top ten relationships in life or clients in business. By doing so, you will strengthen the relationship and encourage others to live a more fulfilling life.

As you close the pages of any of the books in this series, you will gain a new life of clarity and focus as never before. *Cracking the Rich Code* will provide tools to transform results for corporations, institutions, and individuals, both personally and financially.

If you've ever wanted to read a book that challenges you to become more than you are and leaves you with enough inspiration to last a lifetime, *Cracking the Rich Code* is it!

Allow all you have read in this book to create introspection and redirection if required.

Remember, death is certain. Success is not. This life is your journey to craft.

Brian Tracy

Table of Contents

PREFACE vii
Foreword by Brian Tracy xi
Jim Britt 1
    Think Like Superman
Elke Philips 15
    Resiliently Pursuing My Purpose
Raeanne Lacatena 27
    The Power of Perspective: Overcoming Business Obstacles
Katie Augustine 40
    An Evolutionary Birthing: A Perspective on Personal Development as part of Collective Evolution
Raymond Michael Rivera 52
    The Devil Inside of Us
Karen Justice 64
    Hero Mapping
Smita Das Jain 78
    Destiny by Design: The Empower Yourself Blueprint to Success

David Radosevich, Ph.D. **90**

    Neuro-Leverage: Your Brain's Unstoppable Formula for Success

Julie Hruska **104**

    "Generating Wealth: Transforming Limiting Beliefsby Cultivating an Abundance Mindset"

Baz Porter..**122**

    The Phoenix Rising: How I Transformed My Greatest Pain into My Life's Purpose

Susy Francis Best..**130**

    Cracking the Rich Code: 7 Habits for Holistic Wealth

Kim Malloy, Ph.D...**144**

    Tackling Self-Doubt from the Inside Out

Victor Bullara **158**

    I Will Know It When I See It

Mary Hunter...**172**

    The FORECAST Model: Building Elite Teams That Win

Adriana Gattermayr **186**

    Strength and Honor: Whatever Happened to Empowering Teams?

Yarona Boster **196**

    The Investment Every Parent Needs to Make

Alba Contreras Rodriguez, MBA, PCC

    Use Your Strengths to Enrich Your Life, Not Sabotage It

Andrew Franseen...**220**

    The Craft of Conflict: Do to others as you would like them to do to you. -Jesus

Deborah Kaler **236**
  Dare To Hope Again!
Suzanne Sullivan **246**
  Lightening Leadership –The Secret Code is 360
Rebecca & James Lockwood **262**
  Our Ambitious Journey - "It was going downhill fast."
Afterword **277**

Jim Britt

Jim Britt is an award-winning author of 15 best-selling books and ten #1 International best-sellers. Some of his many titles include Rings of Truth, Do This. Get Rich-For Entrepreneurs, Unleashing Your Authentic Power, The Power of Letting Go, Cracking the Rich Code and The Entrepreneur.

He is an internationally recognized business and life strategist who is highly sought after as a keynote speaker, both online and live, for all audiences.

As an entrepreneur Jim has launched 28 successful business ventures. He has served as a success strategist to over 300 corporations worldwide and is one of the world's top 50 most influential speakers and top 20 life and business success strategist. He was presented with the "Best of the Best" award out of the top 100 contributors of all time to the Direct Selling industry.

For over four decades Jim has presented seminars throughout the world sharing his success strategies and life enhancing realizations with over 5,000 audiences, totaling almost 2,000,000 people from all walks of life.

Early in his speaking career he was Business partners with the late Jim Rohn for eight years, where Tony Robbins worked under Jim's direction for his first few years in the speaking business.

As a performance strategist, Jim leverages his skills and experience as one of the leading experts in peak performance, entrepreneurship and personal empowerment to produce stellar results. He is pleased to work with small business entrepreneurs, and anyone seeking to remove the blocks that stop their success in any area of their life.

One of Jim's latest programs "Cracking the Rich Code" focuses on the subconscious programs influencing one's relationship with money and their financial success.

www.CrackingTheRichCode.com

Think Like Superman

By Jim Britt

"Waking up to your true greatness in life requires letting go of who you imagine yourself to be."

--- Jim Britt

FACT: Becoming a millionaire is easier than it has ever been.

Many people have the notion that it's an impossible task to become a millionaire. Some say, "It's pure luck." Others say, "You have to be born into a rich family." For others, "You'll have to win the Lotto." And for many, they say, "Your parents have to help you out a lot." That's the language of the poor.

A single mother with five children says, "I want to believe in what you're saying. However, I'm 45 years old and work long hours at two dead-end jobs. I barely earn enough to get by. What should I do?"

Another man said, "Well, if you work for the government, you cannot expect to become a millionaire. After all, you're on a fixed salary and there's little time for anything else. By the time you get home, you've got to play with the kids, eat dinner, and fall asleep watching TV."

Everyone has a story as to why they could never become a millionaire. But for every story, excuse really, there are other stories OR PEOPLE with worse circumstances that have become rich.

The truth is that all of us can become as wealthy as we decide to be, and that's a mindset. None of us is excluded from wealth. If you have the desire to receive money, whatever the amount, you have all of the rights to do so like everyone else. There is no limit to how much you can earn for yourself. The only limitations are what you place on yourself.

Money is like the sun. It does not discriminate. It doesn't say, "I will not give light and warmth to this flower, tree, or person because I don't like them." Like the sun, money is abundantly available to all of us who truly believe that it is for us. No one is excluded.

There are, however, some major differences between rich and poor people. Here are some tips for becoming rich.

Change Your Thinking

You have to see the bigger picture. There are opportunities everywhere! The problem is that most people see just trees when they should be looking at the entire forest. By doing so, you will see that there are opportunities everywhere. The possibilities are endless.

You'll also have to go through plenty of self-discovery before you earn your first million. Knowing the truth about yourself isn't always the easiest task. Sometimes, you'll find that you are your biggest enemy—at least some days.

Learn from Millionaires

Most people are surrounded by what I like to call their "default friends." These friends are acquaintances that we see at the gym, school, work, local happy hour, and other places. We naturally befriend these people because we are all in the same boat financially. However, these people aren't millionaires in most cases and cannot help you become one either. In fact, if you tell them, you will become a millionaire, some may even tell you that it's impossible and discourage you from even trying. They'll tell you that you're living in a fantasy world and why you'll never be able to make it happen. Instead, learn from millionaires. Let go of these relationships that pull you down regarding your money desires. It's okay to have friends that aren't millionaires. However, only take input from those who have accomplished what you want to accomplish. Hang out with those who will encourage and help you reach the next level. Don't give your raw diamonds to a bricklayer to cut.

Indulge in Wealth

To become wealthy, you must learn about wealth. This means that you'll have to put yourself in situations that you've never been in before.

ON OCCASION, DO SOME OF THESE:

Fly first class and see how it makes you feel.

Eat out at the finest restaurant, and don't look at the price on the menu.

Take a limo instead of a cab or Uber. Watch how you feel.

Reserve a suite in a first-class hotel.

If you are used to drinking a $20 bottle of wine, go for the $100 and see how it tastes. It does taste different.

All I am saying is, try some things that wealthy people do and see how it makes you feel.

Believe it is Possible

If you believe it is possible to become a millionaire, you can make it happen. However, if you've excluded yourself from this possibility and think and believe that it's for other people, you'll never become a millionaire.

Also, be sure to bless rich people when you can. Haters of money aren't likely to receive any of it either.

Read books that millionaires have written. By gaining a well-rounded education about earning large sums of money and staying inspired, you'll be able to learn the wealth secrets of the rich. I just saw a video on LinkedIn with my friend Kevin Harrington from the TV show Shark Tank. He said that one of his new companies just had a million-dollar day on Amazon.

Enlarge Your Service

Your material wealth is the sum of your total contribution to society. Your daily mantra should be, *'How do I deliver more value to more people in less time?'* Then, you'll know that you can always increase your quality and quantity of service. Enlarging your service is also about going the extra mile. When it comes to helping others, you must give everything you have. You just plant the seeds, and nature will take care of the rest.

Seize ALL Opportunities That Make Sense

You cannot say "No" to opportunities and expect to become a millionaire. You must seize every opportunity that has your name on it. It may just be an opportunity to connect with an influential person for no reason. Sometimes the monetary reward will not come immediately, but if you keep planting seeds, eventually, you'll grow a fruitful crop. Money is the harvest of the service you provide and sometimes the connections you have. The more seeds you plant, the greater the harvest.

Have an Unstoppable Mindset

Want to know some of what my first mentor shared with me that took me from a broke factory worker, a high school dropout, to a millionaire?

First, he said, you must start thinking like a wealthy, unstoppable person. You must have a wealth mindset. He said that wealthy people think differently. He said, "I want you to start thinking like Superman!" Sounds crazy, right? Well, it's not. It's powerful, and here's why. How you think will change your life.

Wealthy people think differently. They really do. And anyone can learn to think like the wealthy.

I'm not talking about positive thinking, the Law of Attraction, or motivation. Let's get real. None of that stuff works anyway. Otherwise, we would all be prosperous and happy already.

Instead, I'm talking about thinking based on quantum physics. Once you understand and apply it, it will change your life. You will become unstoppable!

If there was any fictional or real person whose qualities you could instantly possess, who would that person be? Think about it. Personally, I would say that Superman is the perfect person. Now, you are probably thinking I have lost it, right? Just stick with me here. You will like what you are about to hear.

Superman is a fictional superhero widely considered one of the most famous and popular action heroes and an American cultural icon. I remember watching Superman every Saturday morning when I was a kid. I couldn't get enough. He was my hero!

Let's look at Superman's traits:

Superman is indestructible.

He is a man of steel.

He can stop a locomotive in its tracks.

Bullets bounce off him.

He is faster than a speeding bullet.

No one can bring him down.

He can leap tall buildings in a single bound. Great powers to have in this day and age, wouldn't you say? What else would you need?

Now, for all you females, don't worry. We have not left you out. There is also a female version of Superman named Superwoman. She has the same powers as Superman.

Now, this is where it gets interesting. Let's first look at the qualities that Superman possesses that you want to make your own. And to make it simple, I will refer to Superman for the rest of this message, and you can replace him with Superwoman if you are female.

Again:

Superman is powerful and fearless.

Superman is virtually indestructible—except for kryptonite, of course.

Superman can stop bullets.

Superman has supernatural powers. He can see through walls.

Superman can stop a speeding locomotive.

Superman can stop a bullet.

Superman jumps into immediate action when troubles arise.

Superman can crash through barriers.

Superman can even change clothes in a phone booth in seconds. Not too many of those around anymore. You'll have to duck behind a building to change.

So, you're thinking right now, *'Okay, I know that Superman has incredible supernatural powers, how can that help me? What good will it do me to think I am Superman, a fictional character?'*

Here is where science comes in. This is the part where you will be amazed when you learn about the supernatural powers you already possess! NO, REALLY!

Your brain makes certain chemicals called neuropeptides. These are literally the molecules of emotion, like love, fear, joy, passion, etc. These molecules of emotion are not only contained in your brain but circulate throughout your cellular structure. They send out a signal, a frequency much like a radio station sending out a signal. For example, you tune in to 92.5, and you get jazz. Tune in to 99.6, and you get rock. And if you are just one decimal off, you get static. The difference is that your signal goes both ways. You are a sender and a receiver.

You put out a signal, a mindset of confidence about your financial success, and people, circumstances, and opportunities show up to support your success. When you put out a signal of doubt and uncertainty, you receive support for your doubt and uncertainty. You've been around someone you didn't trust or felt less than positive just being in their presence, right? You have also been around people that inspire you. That's what I'm talking about. You are projecting a frequency, looking to resonate with the frequency you are transmitting.

Anyway, the amazing part about these cells of emotion is that they are intelligent. They are thinking cells. These cells are constantly eavesdropping on the conversation that you are having with yourself. That's right. They are listening to you! And others are listening to your cells as well. Others feel what you feel when they are around you.

Your unconscious mind and cells are listening in, waiting to adjust your behavior based on what they hear from you, their master. So just imagine what would happen if you started thinking like Superman or a millionaire.

Here are some of the thoughts you might have during the day:

"The challenges I face today are easily overcome, after all I am Superman."

"I am indestructible."

"I have incredible strength."

"Nothing can stop me...NOTHING."

"I have supernatural powers and can overcome anything."

"I can accomplish anything I want when I put my mind to it."

"I can break through any barrier."

"I can and I will do whatever it takes to accomplish my goal."

"I fear nothing."

The trillions of thinking cells in your body and brain listen, and they create exactly what you tell them to create. Their mission is to complete the picture of the you they see and hear when you talk to them. They must obey. It's their job!

Since you are Superman, you cannot fail. Why? Your thinking cells are now sending the proper signal because you told them to. They are making you stronger and more successful every day! You have the ability to fight off all negativity, doubt, fear, and worry—nothing can stop you!

Superman has total confidence. So, your cells of emotion relating to confidence will now create more neuropeptide chemicals to promote feelings of power and confidence that others will feel in your presence.

Superman is fearless. So, your cells of emotion relating to fear will now create more neuropeptide chemicals to create feelings of courage. You are unstoppable!

And here's the key. Others will respond to you in the same way that you are talking to yourself.

If you are confident, others will have confidence in you.

You have thousands of thoughts every day. Make sure your thoughts are leading you in the direction you want to go. Ensure you tell your cells a success story and not a 'woe is me' story.

Most have been conditioned to think that creating wealth is difficult or only for the lucky few. What do you believe? It doesn't cost anything to think like Superman, and it is much more inspiring!

Mediocrity cannot be an option if you decide to be wealthy and think like Superman.

Your decision and communication with your cells create a mindset; that influences how you show up.

None of that old type of thinking matters anymore. After all, you are Superman, and you can accomplish anything.

If you want wealth, you have to stretch yourself. You have to do the things that unsuccessful people are unwilling to do. You have to say "yes" to an opportunity, then figure out how to get the job done.

Maybe you are uncomfortable selling and asking for money. If that's the case, then learn sales and learn to ask for money every day until you feel comfortable asking for it. You will never have money if you don't learn to ask for it.

I've learned a lot in the past 40+ years as an entrepreneur. I've learned that in order to have more, you have to become more. I've also learned that if you are comfortable, you are not growing. I realized that I couldn't go from being a nervous rookie speaker with minimal self-confidence to hosting TV shows and speaking in front of 5,000 people overnight. I simply wasn't ready. I grew into that, one speaking engagement at a time. Every time I finished a speaking engagement, I would ask myself, "How did I do it, and how could I do it better?" I still do that today.

And I've learned from the hundreds of thousands of people I've trained, coached, and mentored that none of us can do something we don't believe is possible. It won't happen if you're not ready to step out of your comfort zone and stretch yourself.

This has led me to understand the most important principle of wealth-building, which has meant the difference between poverty and riches for people since humans first traded for pelts.

Are you ready?

Come in just a little closer. Listen up!

Every income level requires a different you, a different mindset! If you think that $10,000 a month is a lot of money, then $100,000 a month will be completely out of reach. If you believe that having $5,000 in the bank would make you rich, then $50,000 won't miraculously appear. You will never earn more money than you believe is "a lot" of money.

What you do as a business is only a small part of becoming rich. In fact, there are thousands, if not tens of thousands, of ways to make money—and lots of it. I've learned over the years that focusing on who you want to become instead of what you need to do will multiply your chances of getting rich a hundredfold.

Ask anyone who's found a way to make a large sum of money legally, and they will tell you that it's not hard once you crack the code. And cracking the code starts with you and your mindset. The "code" I refer to isn't a secret rite or ancient scroll. It's not even a secret. It's a certain way of thinking and believing in which you've trained your mind to see money-making ideas.

That's where you see a need in the marketplace and jump on the idea quickly. It might involve creating a new product, or it may just be teaching others a special technique you've learned. It may even require raising capital to start a company or to market a product or idea on social media.

Don't Hold Back. You Have to Take Action to Change.

Start right now to imagine yourself as already having wealth. How would your life be? How would your day unfold? Start to own your wealth mindset now! The subconscious mind is unable to differentiate between fact and mere visualization. So, by imagining that you already have it, you're encouraging your subconscious mind to seek the ways and means to transform your imaginary feelings into the real thing.

Find yourself some mentors. Nobody has all the answers. Surround yourself with people who will support, inspire, and provide solutions that keep you moving in the right direction.

Having a qualified mentor is essential if you genuinely want to attain wealth, have a thriving business, or reach the top of your game in any endeavor.

Okay, let's come in for a landing…

Having a crystal-clear picture of what you want to accomplish is essential before you begin. If you want to attain wealth, you must learn to operate without fear and with a sharply defined mental image of the outcome you want to attain. This comes from thinking like a wealthy person (like Superman), making decisions like a wealthy person, and being fearless (like Superman) when stepping out of your comfort zone. Look at the result as something you're already prepared to do; you just haven't done it yet.

Think about this. You have been preventing your success; it's not something you have to struggle to make happen. The key is not letting fear, doubt, other people, or mind chatter push your success away. You'll find that the solutions taking you toward your goals will come to you in the most unexpected and sudden ways. You don't need the *perfect* plan first. You need a perfectly clear decision about your success, the right mindset, mentoring, and the ideal way to get you there will materialize.

The most significant transfer of wealth in the history of the human race is happening right now. Are you positioned to get your share?

Remember, in order to get a different result, you must do something different. In order to do something different, you must know something different to do. And in order to know something different, you have to first suspect that your present methods need improving.

THEN, YOU HAVE TO BE WILLING TO DO SOMETHING ABOUT IT.

***

To contact Jim:

For more information on Jim's work:

www.JimBritt.com

http://JimBrittCoaching.com

www.facebook.com/jimbrittonline

www.linkedin.com/in/jim-britt

For free audio series www.RichCode1.com and www.RichCode2.com

Elke Philips

Elke Philips is a career and executive coach driven to guide individuals through career transitions and professional pursuits. She raises awareness around innate talents and interests to ensure individuals pursue an optimal career. Elke is particularly motivated by maintaining a resilient life.

She has expertise in corporate and non-profit environments across industries, through various human resources and career coaching roles, developing and coaching individuals, recruiting, driving employee relations, and facilitating leadership events.

Currently, Elke coaches' individuals in career transition across industries on topics including personal branding, career exploration, resume writing, interviewing, new role success, and overall development. She is also well-versed in leadership and personality assessments, including Hogan Leadership. Previously, she has facilitated career development workshops, written content, and hosted career events and executed optimal career development strategies to ensure swift job placement.

Elke obtained her Board-Certified Coach (BCC) credential from the Center for Credentialing and Education (CCE), an Associate Certified Coach (ACC) credential from the International Coaching Federation (ICF) and completed a life coaching program at the Institute for Life Coach Training (ILCT). Additionally, she earned a master's degree in counseling from Seton Hall University.

Resiliently Pursuing My Purpose

by Elke Philips

On a rainy afternoon in the suburbs of a Western European community, a young girl stood in front of the mirror, pondering infinite possibilities reflecting back at her. Little did she know that this moment, where the world seemed both vast and uncertain, would be the start of a journey - one marked not only by the choices she made but also by the resilience she discovered within herself. Although she felt lucky to be able to consider various professional choices and opportunities, she felt overwhelmed by the prospect of having to choose one path without feeling scattered. Would she like to become a photographer? How about a psychologist? It all sounded exciting. In those days, career advice was hard to come by for youth. Although she had many interests, one constant always seemed to find her consistently: friends knocking on her door in need of help solving a problem or longing for counsel about their early life challenges. She was born an innate helper at heart – regularly dropping everything to listen to others' predicaments. This was never a burden for her – on the contrary. Contributing to someone's growth by creating insight and awareness made her feel purposeful and *rich*. She did not yet recognize then that her natural ability to listen and empathize was a pillar for a potential career in the helping professions. They were just a natural flow of life to her and something she considered an innate state of being rather than a career choice. Throughout her childhood and beyond, she navigated through the storms of confusion with a growing realization that unwavering resilience would be necessary to create success in her career and life.

Many moons later, I still have fond memories of that girl – *me in my early days*. I learned that marrying what I enjoy the most with what I'm innately good at could be a formula for success. Fueled by a career I love, I continue my streak of guiding people to advance their lives and careers – whether to build upon individuals' current circumstances or co-create new prosperous dream careers. This has become my mission. As a career and executive coach, I feel most energized when resiliently living my life *on purpose* through providing guidance in career, professional, and personal development. To my core, I believe that if you can spend time on what makes you happy and fulfilled through a resilient lens, you are abundant – *you cracked the rich code*.

Yet, how did I get there? One would think it is simple to follow one's purpose – *just do it*. Right? For some, it is that easy. Yet, for others, it is a struggle of unclarity or resistance from others. Choosing a particular path might not be popular, adding a complex layer to the dilemma. This will require seeking the power from within to face outside resistance to pursue the unpopular or deemed impossible track. Some of us self-sabotage and resist creating a career that, from the onset, was clearly the right fit for us, yet one we could or would not embrace. I signed up for a career detour first while self-reflecting and realizing what I didn't want by the process of elimination. Sometimes, reaching life and career goals that are authentic to you means going back to school, moving to the other side of the world, combining a side hustle with another full-time job, and splitting time between a family unit and studies. It might demand persistence and tenacity. Regardless, it is an exciting journey well worth the trek!

What probably led you to this book is the desire for abundance – whether it is riches in love, finances, wellness, or building a purposeful career that could leave a legacy. My interpretation is that the rich code is a barometer that can continuously be tweaked. We're constantly in flux between richness in finances, wellness, happiness, and relationships, which means everyone's richness across these areas can vary according to our phases of development. Flux and re-evaluation are helpful to arrive at the best outcome, yet they require resilience! It is the ability to flex and bounce back like a rubber band as changes or perceived challenges occur. It is the mental agility that keeps us going strong. Without resilience, I'd be walking a path ungrounded. External circumstances can throw a wrench in plans and test us to our core. Some of us are parents, helping professionals, homeowners, or individuals with numerous responsibilities to consider. It is safe to say that we allow distractions to get in the way of building our best career and life, especially if we're conditioned to think that juggling responsibilities and merely surviving can be tricky enough, let alone trying to thrive in career and riches. Whether your rich code is becoming a stay-at-home parent, building a business, or aiming for an executive role, one of the aspects that will help accelerate this process is building, improving, and maintaining resilience over time. I've seen firsthand how building the ability to bounce back from setbacks can make the difference between merely surviving or thriving.

I'd like to share a few elements that have been the most helpful for me in increasing my resilience in the face of adversity while building my career to stay abundantly energized. After all, as a parent, I often find myself having to juggle everything at once. I had to learn that being kind to myself is imperative. Every day was, and still is, a new opportunity to navigate challenging encounters resiliently.

Your Mindset: Acceptance and the Silver Lining

"Peace came over me when I realized the door wasn't opening because it wasn't my door to begin with, and a better door was yet to appear."

Change is not always easy to process, yet it lures around every corner. It is constant and requires swift adjustment to external circumstances by flexing a muscle that might be underused. It was easy to feel sorry for myself when unjust circumstances happened in my career or life in general. You didn't get the job, the loan, the promotion. As financial pressures mounted along with needing to provide for a family, stress built along with questions such as "Why me?" or "Why do I need to endure all these challenges?". I never felt comfortable in self-deprecation, though, and would feel a sense of guilt when complaining. What good would it do? It took me many years to realize that things don't happen TO me. They happen FOR me. There is ALWAYS a silver lining.

Observing the discomfort of change turned me into a chameleon of sorts. Over the years, although I could embrace change, I didn't entirely understand what acceptance meant. I thought acceptance translated into agreeing with current reality and actions. Yet, to the contrary, acceptance means we understand, are aware of, and accept the current reality without necessarily agreeing with it. I realized it was time to make lemonade with lemons. From this point of awareness, I could now move to where I needed to go. After all, if we were to stay in our comfort zone, or if no obstacles were ever thrown in our path, would we have taken the necessary steps in our personal lives or careers that create the massive change essential to growth? It is a well-known fact that diamonds are made under pressure. The silver lining is that if changes or seemingly unfortunate events happen, we can start rebuilding our next chapter in ways we could not have imagined otherwise. From coaching people in transition, merging from one phase in their career to the next, plenty of them look back after what seemed to be a rollercoaster ride of a job search and can't help but feel grateful for the positive changes that have emerged. Gratitude as a lens through which you see the world is a splendid tool for keeping a positive perspective. Although transition requires a certain amount of processing and re-evaluation of the next steps in career and overall circumstance, more significant leaps are made towards growth at times of great change. Think about the caterpillar turning into a butterfly or the brightest new business ideas coming out of times of crisis.

Clarity & Understanding Yourself

"It suddenly clicked after brainstorming around my values and areas of expertise and putting pen to paper on some of these keywords to turn them into MY narrative."

Many of us were not conditioned to think or talk about ourselves regarding *personal brand*. Yet, who are we really to the core? Understanding ourselves is a main ingredient in building our roadmap. It creates clarity and confidence that fuels our next steps in the right direction. Knowing who we are, what we are innately talented in, and what makes us happy creates needed clarity that provides the tools to remain confident when we need it the most. My trick was to picture myself at my happiest at work or in general and, consequently, ask myself what I was doing at that moment. What made me smile and feel satisfied? What was it that made me feel content and excited? Visualizing satisfactory moments wasn't the hardest for me – it was building a story around it that eloquently represents me. An exercise that helped start the process was finding words describing my values, skills, and daily functions. We might unconsciously know ourselves well, yet often, it is not until we verbalize our narrative that *our brand* becomes clear. The more I say things out loud, the more I realize who I am *authentically*. Apart from manual exercises such as the latter, of course, there are many assessments on the market to get to know oneself better as a professional or person overall. Awareness of oneself is critical. Once I understood myself better, it became easier to grow confidence and dodge obstacles.

Focus Through a Mindful State

"When I fully experience the present moment, I can focus and gain clarity – the past is gone, and the future has not yet arrived."

I find focus within the present moment. It is an imperative element to actively organize myself towards concrete steps. In the past, not operating from a mindful state kept me from taking certain steps ahead. Fear would stop me in my tracks, and thoughts of problematic future outcomes took a front seat. When we live in the past or the future, we cannot focus on what's right in front of us in the NOW. This seems like a straightforward notion, yet countless times, I have caught myself floating back to the past or worried about the future. It is difficult to focus and move ahead with goals when we are not mindfully here, in the moment. Scattering attention between the past and future drains our resilience – a distraction that can cause confusion. Since the only time that exists is *now*, paying attention to our needs while planning the following milestones is like moving along with the stream rather than swimming up against the current. Embracing a mindful state can be developed. It can be practiced in the smallest of tasks throughout the day. For instance, paying attention to the water flowing off my hands when I wash them, looking at the texture and lightness of the leaves as they blow in the wind, smelling the scents of nature as I walk through the park, feeling the texture of my blanket as I sit on the couch. There are many opportunities to be mindfully present in every part of our day. What senses would you utilize to be observant in the moment?

Confidence & the Imposter Syndrome

"Who am I to coach or write a chapter on this topic? Oh – how these intrusive thoughts rang true for me!"

So many experts have written books on similar topics before, so what makes me special? The imposter syndrome has followed me for a significant portion of my life. It is the notion that even when realistically well-versed in your craft, there is a sense of doubt whispering you might just not be suitable or knowledgeable enough. Feeling like an imposter cast a shadow and prevented me from reaching certain career heights. Coaching others every day taught me I'm not alone in this boat. I'd have a hefty savings account if I had a nickel for every time a job searcher expressed feeling a lack of confidence at some part of the process. We're all humans, dealing with earthly experiences and emotions. I wish I could say that the flip of a switch turned this around from feeling not confident enough to stepping up and taking leadership. Time, know-how, and experience in my area of expertise have helped tremendously overcome this feeling of "lack" over time. Discussing the topic with peers normalized my experience also. Learning a new skill to further expand your knowledge, even from an hour-long webinar, can boost some of that confidence. It took receiving feedback from others in my field and the individuals I coached to understand the positive impact I was having on them. Also, any mistakes made were used as tools to become better. Is there always more to know and experience to gain? Of course – yet in the meantime, it is imperative to understand that every bit of contribution you provide, even if it is one tiny nugget of improvement or *aha* moment as a takeaway, you made a difference. Giving yourself that pat on the back goes a long way!

Setting Healthy Boundaries

"I wish I was taught early in life the importance of setting healthy boundaries, and how to set them as a standard in career and life in general."

Do you say "yes" when you'd rather say "no"? Do you let others get away with things that they shouldn't? Do you take on too many responsibilities? I've certainly been guilty of this many times over and let people overstep boundaries for various reasons – out of a sense of obligation, people-pleasing, or empathy. I didn't realize that I was slowly chipping away at my energy, motivation, and vision and started feeling like a deflated balloon. Not setting firm boundaries can lead to a full-blown burnout. It is good to give; I came at it from this premise. Yet, ask yourself if what you are giving is within the realm of set boundaries. What are those boundaries? Become aware of what time, money, energy, and resources you can provide before things are no longer balanced. I started thinking more along the lines of what was within my comfort zone to do and within my time and means. When I began taking inventory, I came to staggering conclusions that I gave more than was energetically possible. Remember, though, that saying "no" does not mean it will be a "no" forever. Perhaps reframing that at some point in the future, you could consider doing *xyz*, however, at this very moment, there are other commitments – whether to others or yourself – that must take precedence. Once I started practicing setting clear boundaries, I was surprised by people's immediate and long-term reactions. Some showed their true nature by resisting and lashing out in response to my clear boundary-setting; some thought I suddenly became "difficult". The right people in your circle, though, will respect your healthy boundaries and the notion that you are on your way to solid self-preservation and resilience.

Play and Self-care

"How much can I pour in others' cups, if my own cup is empty?"

When searching for the best scenario to balance a career I love while raising my children, I knew it was imperative to remain a strong rock they could depend on. I mastered the juggling act, gained clarity about my professional identity, and was aware of my beliefs and abilities while being able to organize my daily agenda. However, an underestimated element needed to lead a fully resilient life was missing - the element of play and self-care. Without filling my own cup, how could I operate? How could I have enough battery life to help everyone around me without nurturing myself? I knew it was essential to take care of myself and understood that you must first put your oxygen mask on before helping others. What good am I when drained or headed for burnout?

Nevertheless, putting what I knew into practice was a challenge and a half! I think we've all experienced saying, "yeah, I want to do that for myself, but..." and nevertheless don't follow through on taking care of ourselves, as we *must* take care of other tasks or people first. For years, I struggled with guilt when carving out rejuvenating time for myself. How can I think about doing something fun or simply building in a moment of relaxation while there are many responsibilities to take care of? Little by little, I started allowing myself to enjoy something small. You could look at these actions as baby steps - they could have been as simple as hopping in the car and driving to a nearby town I'd never been to, getting a new haircut, or simply staying on the couch with a blanket to watch a movie. I started scheduling in "me" time, just as much as I scheduled in everything else. As *play* became a list item, it became part of my routine. Today, I allow myself to attend concerts I want to see, visit the countries I want to visit and eat the meals I have been craving for a long time. My simple mindset shift made me realize that doing something for myself, no matter how small, was imperative to recharge. This truly was the missing key that helped me regain enough energy to take care of everyone around me optimally and strive for success. What could you implement today to allow yourself some *you* time?

Building resilience will be your friend while creating your optimal life and beyond. There will always be a new goal to reach. In the process, be kind to yourself and remember the world needs you and your special gift. Go prosper!

***

To contact Elke:

elkephilips@mail.io

www.linkedin.com/in/elke-philips/

Raeanne Lacatena

Raeanne Lacatena is a Certified Professional Coach helping busy professionals and entrepreneurs realize their fullest potential. She achieves this by leveraging her expertise as a Reiki Master, Licensed Registered Mental Health Counselor, and Emotional Freedom Technique practitioner, complemented by her acute empathic abilities and communication skills.

With 20 years of experience as a counselor and over a decade as a business coach, Raeanne empowers her clients to harness their unique talents, curate personalized self-care toolkits, and address any obstacles hindering them from achieving their ideal lives. Her blend of business management, strategic planning, and her knack for unlocking individuals' potential equips her to guide clients' past hurdles and toward success and contentment in various aspects of life, including relationships, finances, communication, health, and wellness.

Raeanne studied psychology, music, and French at Ithaca College and earned a master's degree in advanced generalist practice and programming from Columbia University. Raeanne currently operates as a Holistic Business Coach. Her client base spans the country, serving diverse entrepreneurs as they ascend to higher levels of leadership in their respective industries.

Residing in picturesque western NY with her husband, three young children, and two small dogs, Raeanne and her family share a passion for travel, music, culinary adventures, basking in the sun, and spending cherished moments by the water.

The Power of Perspective: Overcoming Business Obstacles

by *Raeanne Lacatena, LCSW-R, CPC*

It was one of those picture-perfect July days. Jerica, an entrepreneur and makeup artist, was opening a new brick-and-mortar space with her business partner. This wasn't merely a relocation; it marked the realization of their goals and the anticipation of a future rich with opportunities, growth, and financial freedom. This moment signaled the beginning of their next chapter. But what happened next sent Jerica into a spiral that threatened the future of her business.

Jerica had come to me months earlier hoping to reach her highest potential as a business owner. As with every entrepreneur I work with, regardless of industry, I began by helping Jerica develop a business plan and strategy that aligned with her values, mission, and vision. As part of the coaching process, I try to get to the heart of what is really impeding an entrepreneur's success, because I have found it is often more complex than the need for a simple business plan.

This work must be done in every realm of our lives, business as well as relationships, finances, parenting, spirituality, and physical, emotional, and mental wellness. Business success depends on a healthy mindset, a wellness plan, *and* an aligned strategy designed to help the business scale and stretch. Entrepreneurs must understand that who they are anywhere is who they are everywhere, and if they aren't healthy and happy, their business will suffer.

As Jerica's coach, I had helped her develop a business strategy to transition her from an independent makeup artist to a successful production artist working in the entertainment industry. Her 16 years of experience proved to *her* she had the technical skills and talent to make this transition, and through our work, she could see that she had the business acumen as well.

It is my privilege to share this piece of Jerica's story with you in the hopes that whoever is reading this – whatever stage of your entrepreneurial journey you're on – you can identify the situations that make you feel vulnerable and implement the strategies that will move you to a place of comfort and beyond.

On that perfect summer day, the two Latina women arrived at the building eager to obtain the permit they needed to begin business in their new location. At the entrance, three flags supported Black Lives, Trans Lives, and Gay Pride. This put them at ease, knowing they were in the right place at the right time to begin a new and amazing adventure.

They walked into the building and were pointed in the right direction. However, the energy quickly shifted as the permit director and his staff entered the room, stared coldly at Jerica and her business partner, and started to aggressively question them about their intentions. Jerica briefly shared their plan for the new location and was told, in no uncertain terms, that their services were not allowed in that space. When Jerica explained that similar services were operating in the area, the answer did not change. "You are not allowed to provide these services in this area." Jerica felt stunned, helpless, embarrassed, and confused. They discussed some options and decided to contact the realtor and landlord to see if the permit director's claims were true. At this point, the director flushed with anger, handed Jerica his card, told them to have the realtor and landlord call, and then quickly gestured to the door. They could tell this was the end of the conversation and left the building without their permit, feeling deflated and doubting their future.

Jerica had always prided herself as a law-abiding business owner. She operated "by the books." Their current realty team was inviting and ready to make any accommodations to get their business up and running in the best way possible. The day's turn of events filled them with fear for the future of their business and left them wondering how it would make them look in the eyes of their new landlords, realtor, and property management team. Jerica and her partner parted ways wrought with anxiety. When she got home, Jerica reached out to her parents who were livid at the clear racism that their daughter had experienced and encouraged Jerica to fight. This is when the tears started flowing; her fears were confirmed.

There was a voice in her head wanting to stand up for herself, but it was clouded by so many fears and doubts: Could they come after her business or make her and her partner's lives miserable? Was this how it was going to be in this town? Did it mean this space wasn't meant to be? Sadness, worry, anxiety, helplessness, and fear deepened over the next few days as she was awaiting feedback from the realtor. Consumed by these negative thoughts and emotions, she eventually realized she needed help and contacted me for support.

Jerica's situation deeply resonated with me when we spoke. As a social worker by training and a natural helper and protector since childhood, I am triggered by blatant injustices. I believe the world is meant to be colorful and that every race, gender, ethnicity, or diverse human deserves a seat at the table. Diversity makes the spice of life not only more beautiful but also more functional.

We need different perspectives to create more fully. Human beings benefit from the collaborative effort to invite unique perspectives into our work and experiences. When we restrict our access to different human experiences or perpetuate hurtful and unnecessary ways of being, we limit ourselves and deter our healing as a human race.

Over the last twenty years working in personal development, I have created a tool called **STEAR Clear and Anchor.**

Through this evidence-based framework, I help my clients process and reframe their **S**ituation in order to identify alternatives to their current **T**houghts, **E**motions, and **A**ctions that will aid in achieving their desired **R**esults. Then, I lead them through exercises to **Clear** the negative and **Anchor** in the positive.

This framework can completely change the trajectory of entrepreneurs' experiences, businesses, and lives. There will always be challenges to be dealt with in life and business, and this tool has proven effective for all of my clients, from new to seasoned entrepreneurs, striving to achieve greater levels of success. The secret? The strategy remains consistent, no matter what the challenge at hand is.

In Jerica's situation, I began the process by helping her feel her emotions and sort through her thoughts around the permit director's rejection. Using this technique, we identified the **S**ituation, **T**houghts, **E**motions, **A**ctions, and **R**esults related to her challenge and then practiced reframing each category from disempowered to empowered, not-so-useful to more useful, unproductive to productive, or perceived negative to positive.

In the next step, we practiced **Clearing** by releasing and eliminating perceived negative emotions and limiting beliefs associated with the challenge. Then, we practiced **Anchoring** by replacing negative emotions with positive thoughts and feelings, creating a more empowering experience.

Jerica's thoughts and emotions about her current situation were real and justified. I reassured her of this so she could eliminate that level of self-doubt. Creating a space to experience and process those feelings and thoughts was the essence of her healing process. Jerica had been through many experiences in her life when she was judged and mistreated as a Latina woman. This is an unfortunate reality that she faces every day in our society. To suggest that "just thinking differently" about the situation would solve the problem is not creating space for the reality of racism she faced that day, which encompasses the generational trauma that her family has faced.

Grieving reality is important, and acknowledging truth is necessary. This is the first phase of healing after experiencing a negative situation. When we power through these emotions and disengage with the realness of the situation, we run the risk of holding resentment, fear, doubt, and worry in our bodies, which may result in physical inflammation, disease, and often reactive behaviors that do not support our desired outcome.

After facing a challenging circumstance, we either get stuck, shrink and sink into our lower selves, or sail and soar despite the challenge. I see this pattern repeated in both life and business; we choose whether to be stuck, sink, or sail. But before we can choose, we must first feel. Then, we can sort through our thoughts, emotions, and actions to get the desired results based on what's in our control.

Jerica wisely felt her feelings, which created the openness to receive support and validation from her business partner, parents, realtor, coach, and counselor. Eventually, sitting with the negative thoughts and feelings became a burden and counterproductive. That's when she realized she needed a shift.

At this point in her processing, Jerica fully utilized the STEAR Clear and Anchor exercise and realized how much it opened up the possibilities for her.

First, she practiced a brain dump, free association, or traditional journaling exercise in which she wrote everything that happened down on paper. When we write down our experience with pen and paper, we are signaling to our brain that we are externalizing this challenging experience. It's no longer happening. It's a story in our mind that has so much meaning. However, the actual situation is complete for now. This act alone initializes the brain and body to start moving through the upset.

After that, Jerica wrote the letters STEAR vertically down two separate pieces of paper:

"**S**" is for situation,

"**T**" is for thoughts,

"**E**" is for emotions,

"**A**" is for actions, and

"**R**" is for results.

Then she identified the current situation, or the "**S**" in the STEAR acronym. This was simply the present circumstance stripped of all the confounding factors the human brain likes to apply to any given situation. Human beings are meaning-making machines. Before we apply meaning to thoughts, beliefs, ideas, fears, doubts, worries, opinions, past experiences, etc., it's important to get to the core situation, the neutral reality or facts happening right here and right now.

Here is an excerpt Jerica wrote to process her situation and strip it down to the facts and core reality:

"Our space is in a zone that needs approval for our type of service. The head of the permit department needs to approve this just by signing a paper, and he refused." Just the facts.

Then, the next phase in this exercise is to go through the unfavorable thoughts, emotions, actions, and results in each category and replace them with ones we prefer on the corresponding side of the chart.

The first page is where she listed all her disempowered, not-so-useful, perceived negative, and unproductive **T**houghts, **E**motions, **A**ctions, and the **R**esults she no longer wanted, listing the opposites on the second sheet.

There is so much happening when we take the time to do formal thought work. We are separating thoughts from emotions. They are two distinct processes that will follow old patterns and programming without any level of awareness. By understanding the difference between our thoughts and emotions, we can decide how we want to energize the process into action instead of letting it happen automatically.

By recognizing our own tendencies to assign meaning to simple facts, we are having honest conversations with ourselves about how we are behaving and what we can do differently.

We choose our preferred results through productive actions with more supportive emotions and loving thoughts instead of falling into patterns, defaults, or downward negative spirals.

Jerica shared her experience of the process of moving from disempowered to empowered thoughts:

- *"I'm scared he will stop us from moving."* to *"He will not stop me from moving."*
- *"I'm fearful of his power over me."* to *"He doesn't have that much power."*
- *"I'm scared of losing my space."* to *"I am welcomed as a tenant."*
- *"I'm worried that it wasn't the right space."* to *"I'm excited about and comfortable in my new, perfect business home."*

She moved her feelings from sad, worried, stressed, angry, helpless, and anxious to excited, happy, and supported. She also avoided jumping to conclusions and acting on the initial negative feelings in a harmful way such as backing out of her new space in fear of being unwanted or becoming a target in her community. Instead, her confident, empowered, and supported feelings led her to listen to the helpers in her life and ultimately lean into her value as a human, business owner, tenant, and partner. Jerica is now comfortably operating her business in her brand-new business location, against all odds, and couldn't be happier with the decision to move forward and work towards this outcome.

The last two steps in this framework are Clear and Anchor. First, Clear the old, no longer useful thoughts, emotions, and actions by doing whatever is necessary to let them go. Some examples may include taking a walk, getting in nature, exercising, or consulting an expert counselor, mentor, or coach.

For Jerica, she could reach out for support instead of stewing in the emotion alone. Through additional coaching support, she was able to push through her fears and move forward. She said, *"This method enabled me to focus my thoughts around the facts and allow my mind to slow down and comprehend that I would persevere through the situation. My business partner and I were now on track to move into the new space, and emphasizing the positive aspects and support significantly aided in regaining my composure."*

The last step is to Anchor in new, preferred, productive, and loving ways of being, thinking, feeling, and behaving through affirmation, meditation, prayer, and many other approaches depending on the right fit for each individual.

Jerica, like most of my clients, has found comfort in the Emotional Freedom Technique (EFT) or tapping, creating a new environment in her space and business to help her be in an empowered state about this circumstance. As a result, her business is growing, she is on track to step more fully into her new business model, and her new space happily energizes her.

She still has moments when she feels the residual fear arise. However, she is aware of these emotions and can shift them rapidly to a more empowered place. Jerica is excited, feeling safe and supported. She greets each day trusting that she is on the right path and in the right space for her business to flourish. She has found her voice, feels empowered, and will now confidently report that she can stand in her power to protect herself, her business, and her business partner. She is free to evolve the business in any direction and sees the pathway to an incredibly bright future.

Jerica's story shows exactly how this approach works and what occurs during the transformation process. Her story is specific and unique to her situation, but the framework we executed to help her process her emotions is the same for any number of uncontrollable situations that entrepreneurs face.

At the core of STEAR Clear and Anchor, there are a number of psychological, evidenced-based practices supporting the process. This includes free association journaling, cognitive reframing, emotional regulation, mindfulness and relaxation techniques, positive psychology, affirmations, self-coaching, and self-reflection. These tried, tested, and proven techniques are seamlessly woven through the framework. They have improved overall well-being and relationships, enhanced decision-making, increased resilience and self-awareness, improved relationships and communication, decreased stress and increased emotional intelligence, creativity, and personal development.

I truly believe that wealth comes in many different formats. When we are charged with "Cracking the Rich Code," we aren't only discussing how to make our lives and businesses financially successful. More importantly, we are discussing how to be happier and healthier humans who have richer relationships and conversations. We are discussing internal satisfaction and fulfillment in answering our higher calling, loving life, loving people, and unconditionally loving ourselves. The STEAR Clear and Anchor framework creates an easily implementable path for this to be your reality.

While Jerica's experience was personal, STEAR Clear and Anchor can also help with the more strategic, tactical side of business by sorting through the financial and business plans and establishing goals and initiatives. This tool can be used to define a strategy for working towards a TedTalk or landing a book deal or speaking tour. It helps to highlight and celebrate financial accomplishment, become a more present parent or spouse in balance with our business responsibilities, and gain clarity about the legacy of our business. It helps to determine what we value and how to lead a life of fulfillment and significance as well as many more goals the entrepreneurs I work with come to explore.

It can be challenging, complex, and often stressful to build a business and choose the entrepreneurial path, no matter who you are. It is all too common for business owners to face frequent setbacks filled with uncertainties, frustration, and obstacles that can impact their confidence, decision-making, and overall well-being. A tool like STEAR Clear and Anchor offers a very easily implementable technique to discover the most effective path to the happiest, healthiest, and wealthiest life and business possible.

It's my experience that this work can be easy to talk about but difficult to do without the assistance and views of an outside partner.

My purpose is to help entrepreneurs realize and actualize their goals through strategic, holistic coaching. Regardless of your entrepreneurial stage, I encourage you to review my website, where you will find free resources, extended reading materials, additional courses, and comprehensive, high-level coaching for entrepreneurs prepared to take their businesses to the next level.

Are you ready to develop the best version of yourself?

STEAR Clear and Anchor

	Perceived Negative Unproductive - Limiting	Perceived Positive Productive - Empowering
S		
T		
E		
A		
R		

CLEAR

ANCHOR

To contact Raeanne:

www.raeannelacatena.com

https://www.linkedin.com/in/raeannelacatena/

www.raeannelacatena.com/links

Katie Augustine

Katie Augustine has dedicated the last decade of her career to empowering people to live more authentic, purposeful lives. As a Life Mastery Consultant™ and inspirational speaker, she has guided 1000s of clients through personal transformation. Katie's coaching blends spiritual principles with strategic skill sets and action steps. In 2018, Katie joined the Brave Thinking Institute™ as a Senior Coach, encouraging new coaches to establish their businesses.

Katie has been an Earth and animal advocate her entire adult life. Even as a child, Katie loved her backyard swing set in the woods, always feeling connected with nature! This passion led her to become ordained as a Minister of Walking Prayer™ in 2009 with a focus on Indigenous teachings. Katie is also a Maitri Breathwork™ Facilitator, a Reiki practitioner, a social commentary poet, and an attorney. She specialized in risk management as a financial compliance consultant for 22 years.

Katie founded Evolve Consulting Services by merging her ecological interests with her risk expertise. Evolve supports conscious entrepreneurs and organizations in reducing their climate footprint and expenses by implementing sustainable solutions through environmental assessments and frameworks. Katie's mission is two-fold: to support people in living their dreams and to raise awareness for the global collective. She envisions an evolution on our planet in which humanity and the many ecosystems and species thrive in harmony with one another.

An Evolutionary Birthing:
A Perspective on Personal Development as part of Collective Evolution

By Katie Augustine

From the Personal to the Collective

> *"You are not a passive observer in the Universe. The entire Universe is expressing itself through you at this very moment."*
>
> Dr. Jean Houston

It is my humble yet bold opinion that we are in an evolutionary birthing on the planet, and our work supporting others in their personal development is significant as an integral part of collective transformation. I view this extraordinary birthing as a threshold moment for the evolution of humanity and other species on Earth.

Through this chapter, first, I invite you to live your purpose and influence others to live into theirs. The second invitation is to consider the global collective in your work to evolve humanity and all of life on the planet.

Evolution Calling

> *"As within, so without, as above, so below, as the Universe, so the soul."*
>
> Hermetic Philosophy

What if we are on the cusp of an evolutionary tipping point? What if instead of the seemingly overwhelming situations of breakdown, we were on the brink of a breakthrough? What if part of this edge of evolution is dependent on you and your clients stepping into personal greatness as well as envisioning a future for the global collective?

We know scientifically everything is energy, and the Universe is expanding. Science now confirms many theories that metaphysicians of the ages had shared. Ideas such as "thoughts create your reality" have been verified through quantum physics experiments during which the experimenter's expectations affect the projected outcomes.

As the Institute for Sacred Activism founder, Andrew Harvey, shares, *". . . we are in what we could call a quantum situation in which both possibilities of extinction and radical rebirth are simultaneously possible. What quantum physics has revealed is that in every moment what we intend transforms the multiple possibilities . . . that exist in potential."*

Aligned with these truths, we surmise that our very thoughts, expectations, beliefs, and actions ripple through time, affecting our lives, clients' lives, our families and communities, and even the entirety of the planet and the Cosmos itself. We are literally made up of the same particles that forge the stars and the planets; our very life is part of the cosmic expansion. The world is creating itself through each of us. The micro and the macro are one.

What if Source, Energy, God expects each of us to be willing to transform as part of the rising of consciousness? What if it is our responsibility to step into our greatness with a vision for love, harmony, peace, and unity for the global collective, to support the evolutionary birthing of this time?

Courage in the Face of Fear

"We must be willing to be uncomfortable in the interest of growth."

Mary Morrissey

Even as a child, I resisted change. In my early teens, I begged my parents not to move. As I matured into adulthood, I would outgrow a situation and stay longer than served me or the others involved, jobs, homes, relationships. Even after 35 years of personal development and supporting others, I still notice that a part of me would prefer to stay in the "comfort zone."

Working with clients, I'm not alone in resisting change. Resistance is a natural part of growth, and luckily, perhaps, even when we resist, change will occur. It can be a scary, risky yet wise move into the next greater version of life or a grasping and breakdown into another perhaps not-so-great version of life. As the caterpillar knows too well, even if it feels like death, cycles of change occur one way or another!

Each of us will receive the calling to our next version of greatness. Joseph Campbell refers to this as "The Hero's Journey." It starts as a desire or by receiving an idea or an opportunity. Or perhaps we feel pain or notice what's no longer serving us. When we heed the calling despite the fear, we face trials along the way, but ultimately, these tribulations build our capacity to be the next greater version of ourselves. If we don't heed the calling, the knocking gets louder in the form of heartache, anxiety, or even physical symptoms. With awareness and support, we may still rise like the phoenix from rock bottom; this is true for our clients and for each of us.

The alternative is to maintain the status quo, which, in an expanding Universe, actually means to disintegrate and devolve. We see this in humanity around us, giving way to fear, depression, disease, and dysfunction, living reactively to conditions versus making a positive contribution. Or perhaps it means never living a life of true fulfillment aligned with purpose.

As coaches influencing others, clients often come to us confused or overwhelmed, feeling either pulled by longing or noticing the pain of the current life. This is where we can shed light on the Universal call for growth. Supporting our clients through their transformation is courageous work, perhaps even more significant than we realize!

The Cycle Concept

"There are constant cycles in history. There is loss, but it is always followed by regeneration. The tales of our elders who remember such cycles are very important to us now."

Carmen Agra Deedy

As a person who helps others with their growth, you likely further an awareness with your clients that life is often lived in patterns, inherent or inherited, influenced by society and culture. Growth comes by breaking free of the current pattern into a new, more empowered pattern. Awareness of the pattern or cycle we are in can support the shift into the next phase of the cycle. Cycles apply personally and collectively.

A cycle I share as a metaphor for this time is the birthing matrix founded by Dr. Stanislav Grof, who many consider a primary developer of transpersonal psychology. In his birthing matrix, after gestation and contraction, the next phase in the cycle is the actual birthing (moving through the cervix). The old life is no longer available; there must be an exciting of the womb (current environment) to emerge into the light, which can be scary and messy. However, it leads to the next phase, a rebirth; the baby breathing independently and living at the next and greater version of being-ness.

Collectively, we are moving from a contractive phase into a birthing phase in an evolutionary cycle. Like all birthing moments, this time can be precarious; mothers know the glorious moment of birth comes alongside a risk of death. During this extraordinary time, brave souls come to us for support, sensing that the collective birth is upon us.

The Current Collective Paradigms

> *"Every few hundred years in Western history there occurs a sharp transformation. Within a few short decades, society - its worldview, its basic values, its social and political structures, its key institutions - rearranges itself. We are currently living through such a time."*
>
> Peter Drucker

We feel an undercurrent of something brewing in the collective field. We notice outdated systems are being fought for, for profit, power, or simply out of fear. The threats of nuclear war and environmental collapse are perhaps at the peak of danger in all of time. Instead of bringing brilliant minds together to resolve challenges, we war with each other. Fear propaganda and disinformation sustain old paradigms. Political divisiveness, topped with the Covid-19 epidemic, seemed to have stirred up our nervous systems.

Many clients aren't aware of the reasons but come to us because they recognize something is not quite right. Security seems elusive. Many of us want to find a new normal. Instead, we're witnessing two major wars with children as targets, almost weekly school shootings, and the passing of the 2-degree Celsius global warming threshold. Most of us know, or at least hope, this is not normal.

In the current collective view, however, we're often disconnected to the consequences of our choices and actions. Therefore, we continue to feed unsustainable systems (including governances, products, energies, foods, economic models, wars, etc.) instead of supporting humanity and the regeneration of the planet. Many of us are also under a spell of "busy-ness" and "overwhelm" trying to make it through the day. This sadly seems to provide an excuse to turn a blind eye to situations of atrocities for humans, nature, and animals. However, deep down we know we are at least partially complicit when we allow such atrocities to continue.

Without making light of the destructive situations occurring, these birthing pangs may prompt people to awaken. As Martin Luther King, Jr. said, *"Darkness cannot drive out darkness. Only light can do that."* It is a sacred time for us to support our clients to turn on their lights, despite feeling despair relating to the current conditions.

Many people are waking up and accepting responsibility, demanding better, and wanting to collaborate and contribute to a positive evolution. Therefore, I believe you are being invited to the frontline of sacred work, supporting clients to create a new world aligned with their growth and perhaps aligned with humanity, the ecosystems, and the many species.

Create Coherence for Consciousness

> *"Look at the world around you. It may seem like an immovable, implacable place. It is not. With the slightest push—in just the right place—it can be tipped."*
>
> Malcolm Gladwell

As part of this sacred invitation, I encourage you to believe in the possibility of a collective birthing. We are leaders of an evolving species. As coaches and influencers, we maintain an energetic coherence with the new life evolving out of the chaos, as would a doula for mother and baby. Even amid the pain, fear, and chaos, we may prepare ourselves and our clients for the mystery and magic that is about to be born.

According to Dr. David Hawkins' research (see <u>Power v. Force</u>), true power is an energetic frequency. The higher one moves on the energetic scale, the more impact one will have. For instance, one person at a frequency of 500 (aligned with the state of unconditional love) can impact 750,000 people.

This scientific awareness aligns with messages from enlightened teachers who spoke of the power of thought, consciousness, and coherence. This is why each of us CAN affect this birthing into the next evolutionary phase. Personal growth and transformation raise our energetic frequency and, therefore, tips the collective consciousness.

The new era is not a given; we are at a point of choice. Each person on the planet has free will. But the good news is that only a small number of people are required for a tipping point, which is created through the coherence of energy. Therefore, even if the majority of people continue to conduct their lives in reactive patterns stemming from circumstances, it only takes a small group of us to be coherent with the expansive energy of love to outweigh the masses in fear.

Below is a high-level overview of a process to activate the tipping point. The process includes three steps we may offer our clients for their personal transformation and ultimately, for the collective birthing.

Step 1: Empower

Awareness for Transformation

"There is a secret turning in the heart, which makes the entire Universe turn."

Rumi

As said, everything is energy, and our thoughts and expectations create our current results. Therefore, I am not suggesting we invite our clients to focus on negative news, especially if they are not taking steps to resolve the situation. I am, however, suggesting we are collectively responsible for allowing or participating in outdated and harm-causing systems. In personal development, our work with clients includes an awareness of the patterns they must shift; similarly, it's time to empower our clients to wake up to what's no longer serving the collective.

Many of our client's sense that evolutionary change is underway. While it may be tempting to ignore or suppress the concerns, despair, or overwhelm they feel, the invitation is to support our clients to take another route. Instead, we invite our clients into the pain or discontent of what they see on the planet; and after perhaps experiencing heartache, to consider what they are no longer willing to allow, and therefore where they want to be part of the global change.

We, therefore, empower our clients in an awareness process as part of their empowerment. As Rev. Michael Beckwith of the Agape International Spiritual Center teaches, we remind our clients that conditions are not truth, but simply the limitations we have created. We invite our clients to take steps aligned with possibilities and the energies of peace, unity, love, abundance, harmony, and joy. We empower our clients to want to change!

Those who previously felt despair about making a difference may now awaken with a personal passion. With our coaching they may find their purpose in resolving situations they no longer want to live with, or in creating new systems that obsolete the old. One of my favorite reminders from Buckminster Fuller is, *"You never change things by fighting the existing reality. To change something, build a new model that makes the existing model obsolete."*

Therefore, if perceived and used wisely, the collective old paradigms may be an inherent part of the birthing process, now waking and empowering people to live their purpose, which then ushers in this next great evolutionary time.

Step 2: Envision

Vision and Activate

"You don't get to the dream, you come from the energy of the dream."

Mary Morrissey

After supporting our clients in moving their pain into empowerment, we can lead them through an envisioning process that will support them in taking steps that align with their new passion related to the collective. In personal development, Mary Morrissey, co-founder of the Brave Thinking Institute, asks, *"What would you love?"* This is where we start; Mary's teaching is to create a vision for what you would love and then take action as the person already living in the vision.

Therefore, we invite our clients to create a vision for what they would love in their personal lives, and I suggest for what they would love for the planet and humanity, the ecosystems and the many species. It may be outside their current awareness, but we remind them that love, unity, and peace are possibilities. Perhaps they see regenerative gardens, children feeling safe, social justice and equalities, flourishing creatures, thriving forests and blue oceans! It is not a plan at this level of work; we invite our clients into heart-based dreaming and to hold coherence with their vision.

Then the next part of envisioning is taking action, as would the person in the vision. As a client takes their steps, they will notice resistance. This is when having a structure of support, such as a coach, is essential. Likely, obstacles will rise, and when this occurs, we remind them, as Robert H Schuller said, *"Problems are not stop signs, they are guidelines."* We support our clients to continue to take steps aligned with their vision, regardless of the resistance and obstacles. These steps activate the vision!

Step 3: Evolve

Dare to be Great

"Our deepest fear is not that we are inadequate. Our deepest fear is that we are powerful beyond measure. It is our light, not our darkness that most frightens us."

Marianne Williamson

We invite our clients into their transformation, support them through the obstacles as they align with the vision, and emphasize the significance of their work to the collective during this evolutionary phase change.

As your clients are working on their transformation and feel the pull of resistance, we can ask them: What if you knew that universal evolution at least partially depended on your evolution? Would you dare to be great and brilliant? Would you work through your unworthiness and fears in order to do your part in creating a new world order? Would you be willing to be a midwife for our future generations? Would you be willing to evolve?

As Jean Houston shares, *"We all have the extraordinary coded within us, waiting to be released."* The invitation to yourself and your clients is to release the extraordinary! This is our time to evolve into our greater selves, to support humanity's survival on the planet, and to birth humanity and the many species and ecosystems into a thriving new era on Earth. This is a brave concept and calls for courage. Invite your clients into their greatness and underscore the urgency, for evolution may be hinging on their growth and energetic frequency. It is time for us to evolve!

Conclusion

"When none of these approaches work, you have two directions left. One is despair, cynicism, and apathy, states of mind where a lot of people are right now. The other is empowering people to want to change . . . the kind of change that transforms the whole social system." David Gershon (see Social Change 2.0)

I believe it's beyond time to embrace collective awareness as part of our empowerment and encourage others to do the same. During this evolutionary birthing, there are two paths. If humanity continues in the competitive structures encouraging violence against each other, animals, and nature, we will move into the elimination of life on Earth, as we know it. The other path of collaboration, compassion, and following our callings, leads to the birthing of an age of love, peace, and unity.

As influencers, we can decide to create coherence with the path of evolution by envisioning these possibilities and encouraging others to do the same. As we take steps into our greatness and urge our clients to take theirs, we support the global and perhaps even cosmic collective through this significant birthing moment. This is a time of great crossroads; let's choose courageously and encourage our clients to do the same. As Margaret Mead wisely said, *"Never doubt that a small group of thoughtful committed individuals can change the world. In fact, it's the only thing that ever has."*

***

To contact Katie:

Phone: 1-216-410-3006

LinkedIn: www.linkedin.com/in/katherine-katie-augustine-earthadvocate

Email: Augustinekt@yahoo.com

Facebook: https://www.facebook.com/katie.augustine.16/

Website: ECSevolveconsultingservices.com

Raymond Michael Rivera

A husband and father of two, Raymond Rivera isn't just a thought leader; he's a modern-day renaissance man. Born and raised in the inner city of Chicago's Northwest Side, he's turned life's challenges into victories. As the host of "The Science of Growth Podcast," he doesn't just scratch the surface; he delves deep into the mechanics of personal and business evolution, leaving listeners informed and transformed.

With a Bachelor of Science in Operations Management and an MBA in General Management, his academic prowess is more than a credential—it's a weapon for change. His 15+ years of leadership experience are not just a career timeline but a formula of life-altering impacts. Trained rigorously in Situational Leadership and Operational Excellence, Raymond is not just a decorated business professional; he's a maestro of organizational transformation.

As the author of groundbreaking books, "The Wall Within: Rewiring Your Mind for Success" and "The Circular Continuum: Paradigm Shift Manifesto," Raymond doesn't just write; he ignites revolutions in understanding. As an independent theologian and a Proctor Gallagher Institute graduate, he's not just educated, he's enlightened.

He is not only in the business of incremental change; he's in the business of quantum leaps in personal and professional growth. When he speaks, writes, or leads, you're not just receiving information; you're gaining a blueprint for a seismic shift in your life and business.

The Devil Inside of Us

by Raymond Michael Rivera

The city life was bustling, and the streets of Chicago took on an eerie glow, a blend of flickering streetlights and the misty haze of steam and methane gas rising from the underground sewers. The buzz from passing cars drowned out any natural sounds, leaving me wondering if birds dared to venture out in this unsettling atmosphere.

From the corner of my eye, I noticed a figure in the distance. Their face was downturned, seemingly weighed down by an invisible burden. As I drew closer, the figure materialized into a young boy, his face caked in dry mud except for clean streaks where tears had once flowed. His eyes were fixed in a haunting gaze, unblinking as if he'd seen the unimaginable.

Suddenly, he lifted his head, his pupils unnaturally dilated. That's when I saw them: two gaping holes on his neck, resembling puncture wounds. They looked fresh, the veins underneath exposed yet eerily devoid of blood. He couldn't have been more than ten years old.

The cold air intensified the vapor from my breath, making it almost palpable. A peculiar odor, something metallic, filled the air, adding to my sense of dread. With each step I took, the gravity of the situation began to sink in. More scars became visible on his face, each one captivated me.

"Hey buddy, what's your name?" I shouted from a distance, my voice tinged with curiosity and apprehension. Silence. The boy offered no response, deepening the mystery that hung like a thick fog.

As I inched closer, a bone-chilling realization washed over me: the boy had an unsettling resemblance to someone I knew.

Could it be?

My heart pounded like a drum in a frenzied rhythm, echoing the tension that filled every part of me. Without warning, the boy unbuttoned his coat with deliberate slowness, his eyes never leaving mine. He shrugged off the coat and lifted his shirt over his head, revealing a back resembling a canvas of horror. Scars crisscrossed his skin, each intersecting line accompanied by a tattooed number. A magnetic force pulled me closer; I could not resist, my anticipation reaching a fever pitch.

Just then, the world around us seemed to pause. Streetlights dimmed, and the unrest of city life abruptly silenced. Even the misty sewer vapors hung motionless in the air as if time had stopped. A spotlight from an unknown source illuminated us, casting a weak light on the boy's scarred back.

"What do these numbers mean?" I wondered, my eyes scanning the tattooed dates next to each scar. As I leaned in, my vision tunneled, and a shock wave engulfed me. The numbers were dates, all from previous years.

The boy turned to face me again, his eyes locking onto mine as he pointed to his chest. I gasped. I could see right through him as if peering into a chamber of secrets. His heartbeat within a glassy enclosure, the exterior adorned with icicles, steam swirling around a mysterious keyhole with a padlock.

Finally, he spoke a low whisper that reverberated in the still air.

He replied, "I am the devil inside of you."

Chills ran down my spine.

He continued to gaze into my eyes with a cold stare. Realizing this, I came to a dark revelation.

The boy was me.

The alarm clock buzzed uncontrollably as I opened my eyes.

This encounter serves as a divine revelation and an analogy for the invisible forces that govern our current state and shape our realities in the future. A challenge presents itself to the reader. I will explain this bone-chilling concept and how it catalyzes living a rich and fulfilling life.

But first, after many years of research, I've finally uncovered the master key.

The boy in the story was an archetype and a manifestation of everything that happened to me when I was younger. The holes in the boy's neck were fresh but without blood. This was caused by the energy vampires that I allowed into my life. All types of people, from significant others to leaders and even pastors. Every word they uttered to me was clothed with sheeplike fur, soft to the touch, and void of deception. However, their inner desires were tainted by the deceptive passion for authority and power. A mirror is the only material I can place in front of me, reflecting the shortcomings of a boy victimized by his self-limitations.

Gradually, these vampires dug their fangs inside me, and drained me of all energy.

No blood was left, and every ounce of life force I had as a child was drawn out, even into my early twenties.

My back held the visual deformities of years of discipline. Each painful scar had a date imprinted on it, correlating with a time that I was disobedient. After years of hurt and pain, a chamber developed around my heart. I built it unconsciously and enclosed my heart with a cold reminder that it was now off limits; it was no longer open season on devouring me from the inside out. The process was gradual, a slow disintegration of love and passion, supplemented by screams of condemnation and dissension.

The most striking observation was my face, covered in dry mud, unknowingly losing my purity over the years; the tears that were once present no longer flowed. They were dry for a reason, and I noticed they never were wiped clean. Paralyzed by the fear of rejection, I had no reason to wipe them. I was in a chaotic state, previously devoured by others, mostly self-inflicted, and loosely tied to my need for attention and affection as a child. However, the details of the vision that I saw baffled me. The devil is an external entity, so I thought.

"I am the devil inside of you."

What does that mean?

The character I saw was not only a version of myself but a version of me that I was unaware of. I have come to know this as Paradigm or Metaparadigm.

My book, *The Circular Continuum: Paradigm Shift Manifesto*, states, "A paradigm is a program. The human mind is an operating system. And just like a computer, programs are uploaded and downloaded in the system consciously or unconsciously. You may not have been aware of this concept or willing to have embraced it in the past, but it is undoubtedly true. We did not choose our environment when we were born. We were, instead, dropped into this bucket in the hopes that we would eventually find our way out of it. Some people were dropped in entirely alone, and others with plenty of support. Coincidentally, we all have one thing in common: we are products of our environments. We are all on the same journey in the Continuum. We all eventually come to a point where we find ourselves asking the questions, "Why am I here?" and "What am I here to do?".

The key in the discovery process opened upon the realization that Paradigm was the driving force behind everything I thought, felt, and acted upon. However, throughout my years of searching for spiritual freedom, the sinister nature of its voice made me question everything I thought was real. For this reason, I often wondered. If I were a result of past environmental stimuli and individual thought processes, could

I change my current state by becoming an alchemist? That is, transforming what I perceive as one belief system into another.

The answer was yes.

Summarizing this point, the archetype was my Paradigm, and it was the devil personified as my younger self, still inside of me and holding me back from experiencing the richness of life and fulfilling the destiny that was eluding me every day. As you read this, know that you are not alone. You can conquer this sinister being and control every aspect of it to serve you in the war for success. That's right, it's a war.

We often succumb to thoughts that we are passive observers in this universe, but we are not; we are participators and able to manifest greatness by calling out our paradigms and defeating this devil. Yet, a question arises that encapsulates us all.

What is the devil?

What does this word mean, and how can you defeat this giant?

First, you must be curious enough and keenly interested in the true meaning behind this analogous term. There are two things to consider here: the devil means something different than you think, and we all have the devil inside us. If you cringe at this thought, that is a good first step because the Paradigm within you may be urging you to move away from this chapter. However, you will be introduced to the first law in the battle for your mind.

The words in books are very powerful, containing the prototypes of thought forms from the mind of the infinite, fusing with localized instruments of the divine: you and me. They store the vibrations of spiritual principles, often misunderstood, manipulated, and harnessed like a great lasso holding back the primordial energy within them. But I am unsatisfied fusing with the status quo. My migration through the Continuum ignites my passion for truth. Let's explore this further.

The word "devil" is a modernized version of the Old English word "dēofol," which stems from the word "diabolos." This word is of Greek origin and is comprised of two parts: "Dia-," a prefix meaning "across," "through," or "between," and "bolos" stemming from the verb "ballein," meaning "to throw." The word "devil" stems from the original contextual meaning "to throw across." It doesn't end here, however. The slanderer is more than an external force; I define that voice of doubt and negotiation in The Circular Continuum™.

The devil is the character established by your paradigm, seeking to stop you from achieving your destiny. It is the archetype of anything, or anyone, in your life that stands in your way of preventing the goal from being reached. Yes, the devil is the paradigm accusing you to draw you away from reaching your goal, and "sin" is a choice or decision you make that stops you from reaching it.

A new question arises, however.

What is sin?

Sin is often used in the religious sense, but let's investigate. Like the devil, sin exposes itself in The Circular Continuum™ through your Paradigm. The word sin comes from the Greek "harmartia," which originates in archery, meaning "missing the mark." The underlying spirit behind the word sin is an idea signifying variance versus the goal. I think of it as "devil," the noun, and "sin," the verb. Sin is our actions that directly conflict with the actions necessary for greatness relative to the goal we establish.

In my first book, *"The Wall Within: Rewiring Your Mind For Success,"* I use the word goal as an acronym for "…get out and live." This means that the great distraction in your life, or limiting constraint, that stops you from achieving greatness, is the devil, leading to sin; it is in us all.

We all have sin and a devil leading us to miss our mark consistently. However, that is, until you develop your target and realize the paradigm's existence. It can no longer hide in the basement of your house, deep behind the closed door, screaming your name and echoing in your heart repeatedly.

Once you consciously step out of your comfort zone to examine the details of your past and the inhibitors of your present, you can meet this devil face to face, but you need a goal; you cannot have variance without a goal. The devil and sin will not manifest until your goal is established.

The devil inside of me was my old self. It was a boy with multiple scars, a sad countenance, and roaming the earth in a zombie-like state. I now see all my previous paradigm shifts and transformations as necessary for my personal growth. They were all required to become a qualified teacher on this topic. I learned that the devil and sin were results in my universe and subject to my control. For example, sin was staying quiet if my goal was to say something. The devil was the voice of Paradigm telling me to shut up.

These were all used to prevent me from developing into a new phase in my life, and you probably have experienced, or are experiencing, the same.

If you wish to crack the rich code, you must first uncover the limiting beliefs you have held or continue to hold that are preventing your growth. These points cannot go without proper explanation from the mouth of the great mental scientist himself.

> *"Do not think that I came to bring peace on earth. I did not come to bring peace but a sword.*
>
> *Matthew 10:34*

The sword is division; it is variance, so the paradox within the context of this word remains true. To the Pharisees, Jesus was the devil and was subsequently executed, but to Jesus, the

Pharisees were the devil. Jesus had no sin because the great teacher was always aligned with his target. He never missed his mark in achieving what he set out to achieve; he was fully aware of his connection with the universal power in him and us all.

Therefore, the law of correspondence contains this concept of division as a dividing line between two states and is necessary for the innate multiplying attributes of the divine. Your current and future state is at war, and the first law of combat in the war for success is further described in The Circular Continuum™.

Here is a brief description of Paradigm from the pages of my book, *The Circular Continuum: Paradigm Shift Manifesto*, "The voice of Metaparadigm is communicative and over-explanatory in presenting the reasons for or against any decision. Unlike the intuitive and instinctive action, mutual trust exists between the conscious and unconscious/subconscious/subjective mind. If not controlled, the details involved in a decision cause an over-analysis of all possible outcomes, leading to paralysis and inaction.

The devil is in the details. When it's time to act, don't think; move... the voice of truth within the individual only speaks from a place of expectation. This is inner speech magnified. Since the resolution of Paradigm's experiences is limited to memory, the voice constantly transforms based on the programming induced by the conscious operator.

Resisting the devil, therefore, has become analogous to resisting the voice of the current status quo, leading to the average results that initially caused the desire for change. Resisting the devil is fighting the voice of the past, self-limiting belief, and following the instinctive voice of preparation for the GOAL desired."

In conclusion, you are the master of your own life. However, you may have been a slave to a false belief that you exist in this universe as an outsider. Read this with confidence; you are an active creator. You can step out of your localized self and observe the paradigms you hold, which allows you to crack the rich code.

I can still hear the screams of the boy from afar. The voice is familiar, and the devilish tone changes to a soft sound of despair. He waits in the valley, stretching out his arms and calling out my name. "Raymond!... Raymond. Please help me, I need you, I've always been here to comfort you! You must return to me and show me your face again. Don't leave me down here in this desert. Your family needs you, and I can guide and help you! Please, don't leave me here, I am with you, I love you, please help me, Raymond..."

He is alone, and I left him in the valley of decision. It is that dry, fruitless, and desolate place where no growth exists.

I see something different in the distance, and above the clouds at the top of a mountain, I can see a man with another familiar face. His eyes are like fire, and with a sword in his hand, he reaches toward me as I reach toward him.

The only thing I can do, as I climb vigorously, is listen.

"Hey! Raymond, here I AM...."

The voice sounded familiar, with a distinct tone, exclusively recognizable by my soul and spirit. It was me. The stronger, courageous, passionate, and powerful version of myself.

The richness of truth makes itself known; a monster and a spirit of opulence are awakened in us all when we establish a goal, igniting the beginning of our journey through transformation.

If you're intrigued by the journey from the valley to the mountaintop, I invite you to explore this path further. Tap into The Circular Continuum™, and the devil inside of you will cower in the face of your newfound mastery.

***

To contact Raymond:

https://www.linktree.com/raymondriveramba

https://raymondrivera.me/

Karen Justice

Everyone wants to leave a better planet for our children. Karen wants to leave better children for the planet.

Her background started in fashion, but a near-death experience left her feeling less fulfilled by her apparent success. She changed her focus to making a difference for animals and the environment.

Using her skills as a cartoonist, she captivated the hearts of children and adults alike with her whimsical characters. Her beloved children's books, featuring characters living in the enchanting world of the Florida Everglades, have been likened to the works of Dr. Seuss for their imaginative storytelling and educational value.

Karen is the driving force behind 'The Big Happy Project,' a visionary franchise that merges education, entertainment, and environmental stewardship. Through this endeavor, she aims to instill values of compassion, environmental awareness, and conscious living in children's hearts.

She has paved her path to success by breaking barriers, embracing innovation, and inspiring others to do the same. With a following of thousands, she imparts her wisdom and experience to help individuals achieve personal and financial success.

Karen's work is not only about personal success but also about making a lasting impact on the world. She's on a mission to inspire the next generation of changemakers, teaching them the importance of conscious living, environmental responsibility, and the power of unity.

Hero Mapping

By Karen Justice

A lot of people try to tell God what to do. They talk enough to get their tongues suntanned, but if you want to be of service, you must learn to listen.

Wanting to help others and being effective at it are two different things. I've always cared, but I wasn't always effective. Before I became accomplished at anything, I learned how to receive divine guidance. Now, years later, as a success coach, I've shown ordinary people how to climb goal-oriented ladders and become outstanding—not by mastering manipulative sales techniques, but by opening hearts.

I started life as a shy, withdrawn person, but I can't remember a time when I didn't love animals. I was born on a farm in Canada's wilderness— in remote northern Alberta.

My father had met my beautiful mother while overseas, and like many young women, she'd held a romantic idea of what life in the North would be like. The harsh reality was a difficult transition for her. She was desperately lonely and missed England. There was a great deal of tension between my parents, and as a child, I was aware of it.

I became a worrier, and my anxiety led to stuttering. No children lived anywhere nearby, so I also became withdrawn. My mother did everything she could so I wouldn't be self-conscious about my speech. To get me past my shyness, she'd pretend various animals were writing letters to me. I started watching animals all the time to see which ones were sending the messages. Soon, after constant observation, I could understand their feelings and communicate with them.

I befriended a small group of laying chickens and chose names for each of them. My best friend became a gentle milk cow, who I remember and love to this day.

I was four years old when I learned what would become a foundation for my spiritual journey. One hot afternoon, although I'd been told not to taste the salt lick dad had put out in the pasture for my cow friend, I was lying beside her on my tummy, both of us licking away. When Dad looked up from stooking hay, he shook his head, clumped over, scooped me up, and then, plumping me down on one of the hay bales, he went back to finish up. Finally, he took a long drink of water and settled down beside me.

Sighing, he looked up at the sky, lost in contemplation. Dad had come back from flying for three years in a war; he didn't like to talk about it. He had all kinds of medals, but they held little value for him. He'd given them to me to play with, and I'd quickly lost most of them.

He looked down at me thoughtfully and said, "Never trust organized religions. You can be closer to God in a field like this than in a church. You can talk to God here, and he hears you. If you listen, you'll hear him. It's important that you develop your own personal conversation with God."

That day and his remarks stand out so clearly in my memory. I don't know why he chose to tell a four-year-old something that profound, but I'm so grateful he did.

My father worked as hard as a man can. The North, while starkly beautiful, can be wildly unpredictable. For three years in a row, weather destroyed our harvest. Despite the long, backbreaking hours my father worked, the bank foreclosed, and he lost ownership of our farm.

Finally, in the middle of a blizzard, the day came when we were forced to move. The snow was so high a truck couldn't get in.

We had to pile everything we owned onto a horse drawn sleigh. We made it a few miles before the sleigh tipped. We and all our possessions slid into the deep snow drifts. Even as a child, I knew I'd never forget the desperation and fear on my father's face as he worked to pull us out of the snow, right the sleigh, and reload it before we froze in the howling storm. I also somehow understood that the reason all this was happening to our family was because we lacked something called money.

Sometimes, when discussing my early life, I describe some of the worst times by jokingly telling "poor stories." This one stands out vividly.

Because it was so cold, most of the town kids came to school with thermoses filled with something warm for lunch. I didn't have a thermos, and there was no money for one, so Mom got creative— she put my hot soup in a mason jar, then wrapped it up in two of Dad's lumberjack socks to keep it warm. I had to trudge to school through snow drifts as high as the Pom pom on my wool hat, worriedly lugging a dumb soup-filled sock. As I tried to hurry by, my schoolyard peers would circle me like a yapping dog pack. Since I desperately tried to fit in, they couldn't resist taking a few nips.

We lived on the outskirts of town, and on one of my solitary excursions, I discovered an elderly indigenous woman living in a shack in a field nearby. We became friends, and although she didn't talk much, she loved to talk about plants. She taught me to feel the energy of trees and respect them. I was introduced to the many wonders of a leaf. She showed me wonderment everywhere. Sometimes, she'd simply sit around being interested in me. Her place was shabby, and everything in it was so worn it was gray, but it felt peaceful there, and I loved visiting her.

One day, on the way to her house, I spotted a large, colorful sewing basket on our neighbor's back steps. I don't know what came over me— why I decided to steal it. I crept over, snatched it up, and furtively darted across the field to my friend's shack.

I told her a rabbit had left it for me and I was giving it to her. I was thrilled by how happy she was. No one ever brought her presents, and she loved this sewing basket. I listened to stories of all the sewing she would do, and I basked in her happiness.

The next day, karma bit me on the bum. The neighbor somehow discovered I'd stolen the basket. She grabbed me and made me tell her what I'd done with it. My mother was embarrassed and very upset with me. I watched several women head to my friend's house like a posse of witches to get the basket back.

They were sure she'd put me up to it and forbade me to see her making nasty remarks about Indians. I was so ashamed of what I'd done. It took all my courage to sneak across the field to visit her one last time.

I told her how sorry I was, and without hesitation, this remarkable woman told me she understood. As I looked into her eyes, I could tell that she did. She really did.

Later in life, her memory gave me courage. It helped me realize that acquiring money or material things should never be a person's only goal and that people must examine their definition of success.

Today, I'm thankful for having been poor and grateful that I was a misfit. These and other early experiences helped shape my life— they gave me a dislike of pretentious people who hold themselves above others and taught me to look past people's exteriors and see them for who they really are. Looking back, I realize my friend was a spiritual giant. She helped me become an example of what artist Henri Matisse meant when he said," There are always flowers for those who want to see them."

These lessons helped as I grew older, but I remained timid. We moved a lot, and every year, I had to make a new start at a new school. When I turned 15, something remarkable happened. I'd spent years being an earnest but slightly funny-looking kid with few friends. Almost overnight, that changed. I now found myself the recipient of a different kind of attention. Boys still teased me, but it was because they found me attractive. The scrutiny of what seemed like undeserved popularity made me feel even more vulnerable. But somehow, through the next decade of my life, I gained courage. As we move through life, we grow strong or weak. Courage is often being scared to death, but like any muscle, it gets strengthened by use.

It takes a lot of bravery to start your own business, but I was forced to make that and several other daring choices after the breakup of my marriage. I needed all my courage to start far away from the place that had become my fairytale home in Hawaii. My handsome airline pilot husband had cheated and cared for another woman, but I still loved him. In an effort to put the pain behind me, on a whim, wanting to be someplace I'd feel happy again, I moved to Florida. Unfortunately, with a show of false pride, I'd told him I didn't want anything from the divorce settlement, so I'd left with very little money. I hadn't investigated the viability of the move either. After living in a beautiful home in Hawaii, I now found myself on the verge of homelessness. Wages were so low in most of Florida that I couldn't see myself getting anywhere if I fell into the working-for-minimum-wage trap.

With my last few dollars, I bought just enough supplies to design a few samples of costume jewelry. I'd run so low on funds that I stopped eating consistently, and my weight dropped to 97 pounds, but I was determined. I used my love for exotic plants and animals as my theme and created a wildly romantic collection designed for high-end boutiques.

Nothing felt secure in my life, so attaining financial security would at least create a future for me to move towards. I pushed harder, and from my first sales, I was able to hire several artists to help me. I took a huge chance and invested everything I had earned into a New York trade show.

My designs were an instant and a huge hit. Buyers were lined up at my booth. I signed on one of the biggest hotel chains, several major department stores, and many of the most glamorous boutiques in the country. I was weak with relief that the risk had paid off, but just as the show was wrapping up, the breathless excitement and stress caused my heart to go into a crazy irregular rhythm. I was rushed to the hospital.

I had a series of operations for my heart defect. The third was a drastic procedure to correct a life-threatening deep wound infection. I made it through that final operation, but when I came out of anesthesia, I was told the seriousness of the infection required that I remain in the hospital and that I might not make it.

One pain-filled day, I had a near-death experience. I knew I was dying. I lay in intensive care and talked with God. I was shown the only thing that mattered was love—how much love I'd added to the lives of the people I cared about. I was also shown that I'd come here for a purpose, and that was to open people's hearts to the love of animals. God loves all creatures, not just humans. Animals are souls, too. It was my mission, and my heart ached at the idea of being unable to complete it. I vowed to God that if allowed to live, I'd use any skills I had to make a difference.

But how quickly I forgot once my financial worries resurfaced. As I started getting better, I fell back into fear-based patterns. My company was so new that it couldn't survive without focus for any length of time. I was determined to display a new spring collection at the upcoming New York fashion show. I'd already booked the booth. I had a friend bring me my jewelry-making tools and some of the materials I needed. Propped up awkwardly in the hospital bed, I designed my new spring line.

My doctor worried I'd over-exert myself, but after a few days, I caught him smiling. My determination pulled me along behind it, and despite predictions, I was able to leave the hospital after three weeks.

That tenacity paid off. The media called me an overnight success. Very quickly, I appeared in newspaper and magazine articles, plus on numerous talk shows. My designs not only drew critical acclaim but were collected by celebrities. My work appeared in some of the world's top fashion magazines and on television shows.

I soon had a beautiful home on the water, plus my showrooms on Fifth Avenue in New York, Miami, Dallas, and Los Angeles. However, I found myself feeling less and less fulfilled by my apparent success. I realized that most of what I was doing had only superficial value. What had always been my passion was my love for animals, birds, and the environment, not fashion trends or style. I realized I no longer cared what anyone wore.

One night, I had a vivid spiritual dream. A Manatee was plaintively calling to me while cowering beside my dock on the intercoastal waterway. It was too frightened to return to the safety of deeper water because of all the boats with their churning propellers roaring past. In my dream, I jumped into the water and swam with it while angrily shaking my fist at the boats. When we reached the open water, it turned and gently caressed my face with its fuzzy whiskered snout. I later learned that this is how Manatees sense and caress you. I felt its telepathic communication. Manatees needed my help.

The dream impacted me deeply. I'd fallen in love with that gentle soul. But what was even more powerful happened a week later. That exact dream played out in real life. I helped a frightened Manatee I found huddled at my dock back into deeper water. My heart broke for its plight. I knew God was summoning me and that my life was starting to change.

I decided to write a Christmas story about Manatees. The floodgates opened, and loving inspiration poured in.

At this crossroads, I received several unsolicited letters from two different healthcare professionals working with autistic children. They expressed their wonder that my animal-themed prints and jewelry seemed to touch the children's hearts and caused them to open up— they wanted to know what my characters were thinking.

I was being spiritually guided towards an understanding. I realized today's computer games and morning television programs flash discordant, chaotic imagery. Also, children spend half as much time outdoors as they did 20 years ago. Was it any wonder so many children were becoming hyperactive?

I'd always felt happiest in nature, and that's why, on a marketing trip to Miami, I took the long route through Alligator Alley. It was early morning, and I searched the banks for any sign of alligators. I'd driven this road many times before and had never seen one, but this morning, I was hopeful. Much of the highway has high chain link fencing on both sides so the endangered inhabitants don't become road-kill. Suddenly, a pink spoonbill swooshed down and landed on the fence. All at once, more birds joined it. Quickly, the fence was filled with cranes, egrets, herons, and even storks. Birds of every kind continued to land and watch as I drove past. I noticed dark shapes starting to mass along the riverbank and realized they were gators. As I continued to drive, I saw gator after gator lined up in single file along the shore. I couldn't believe my eyes. I kept blinking to see if I was awake. I was so unnerved I finally pulled into a rest station. I kept thinking that couldn't possibly have happened—but it had. As I sat in contemplation, I realized that I'd been given a 'spiritual waking dream' and was being asked to help the Everglades.

That became a turning point. I closed my fashion business and changed my life's focus. When you offer your service as a channel for source, love flows through you, and you love what you do. Synchronicity and magic happen.

Buckminster Fuller believed strongly that one man can make a difference. He used the analogy of a "trim tab" — a small mechanism that can change the course of an enormous ship or aircraft. On his grave is written "Call Me Trim Tab."

Today's children need hope. Native Americans learned what only the student of nature learns, and that is to feel beauty. They kept their children close to its softening influence.

"We will be known forever by the tracks we leave," is a Native American proverb.

I've been working as hard and as fast as I can. I've already written 11 books in what I've named The Big Happy Flappy Alligator Alley series.

The Big Happy Project is about leaving something beautiful for future generations and making saving the environment lucrative for investors. It's about the Everglades and the Gulf of Mexico. The Everglades was once called Lake of The Holy Spirit by early explorers. The area hangs precariously perched on the edge of our day-to-day world. It's one of the most unique environments on the planet and introduces children to a place of wonder. Groundwaters released from aquifers sustain thousands of Ecosystems. They ripple through places with romantic names – Lake Okeechobee, Paradise Key, Flamingo, Shark Valley, the Gumbo Limbo Trail, and Ten

Thousand Islands. It's the stuff of legend and home to a cast of lovable, colorful characters. In this series, children will be introduced to Gators asleep in their Gator holes, bright pink Spoonbills, the Florida Manatee, Cuban Tree Frogs, Panthers, Indians, and Mermaids. Each character has its own 'big story', and each story deserves a happy ending.

The acquisition of wealth can no longer be the driving force of humanity. Conservation is the most critical issue we face, but traditional ideas are becoming unrealistic. Growing populations and powerful commercial interests are waging war on the environment. Native Americans and environmentalists are found to be fighting a losing battle. Even once protected park land is now becoming endangered. The proposed privatization of Federal Parks presents a frightening picture.

Socrates said, "The secret of change is to focus all of your energy, not on fighting the old, but on building the new."

This project enlists that tactic. The goal involves reclaiming land. Ecotourism is currently growing at a much faster rate than regular tourism. Instead of defeating land development, the goal is to purchase or control these strategic parcels of land and tap into this positive tourism trend. Funding for ongoing acquisitions will be created by merchandising and eventually a new type of 'theme park'—An ever-growing chain of family-oriented campgrounds equipped with guided Eco tours.

Everyone talks about leaving a better planet for our kids. — Let's leave better kids for our planet www.karenjustice.com

I love to underline humor in life's drama, so I've also developed a greeting card line. A smile is the shortest distance between two hearts. Proceeds will be used to help fund the project.

As an artist, I aim to have you carry laughter with you. Laughter is a smile with the volume turned up—it's the fireworks of the soul. It makes life a brighter place. No amount of darkness can hide a spark of light.

We can become our own heroes. We can all make a difference. Rumi stated, "As you start to walk on the way – the way appears."

***

To contact Karen:

www.karenjustice.com

Smita Das Jain

Smita Das Jain, the Founder and CEO of Empower Yourself, is an Executive Coach, Personal Empowerment Life Coach, and NLP Practitioner. An MBA with a corporate background of 14 years advising Fortune 500 companies worldwide, Smita knows people need more than strategies to succeed. Her Empower Yourself Executive Performance Programs empower executives to get better at what they do so that they emerge leaders sooner than envisaged. Empower Yourself Personal Clarity Programs enable busy professionals unhappy in their jobs to transform their passions into professions so that they work because they want to, not because they have to.

An International Coaching Federation accredited PCC coach, Smita has guided >250 middle, senior, and CXO-level leaders across 7 countries in communication, time management, leadership, and career transition matters. *The Asia Business Outlook* named Smita as one of the 'Top 10 Executive Coaches in Asia' in 2022, and *Silicon India* mentioned her among the '10 Most Promising Executive Coaches in India' in 2023. She was also named among India's 'Top 10 Women Entrepreneurs' 2023 by *HerKey*.

A two-time TEDx speaker and a bestselling author of 3 books, Smita has appeared multiple times on national TV channels like *CNBC Awaaz* and *Zee Business*. She has been featured in the world's leading personal development site *Addicted2Success,* and quoted in leading periodicals, including *GQ India*, *The Times of India*, *Fortune India*, *GoBankingRates,* and *MSN*.

Destiny by Design: The Empower Yourself Blueprint to Success

By Smita Das Jain

"Your mind shapes your destiny; choose your thoughts wisely to craft the life you dream."

- *Smita Das Jain*

In 2019, I found myself standing at the crossroads of uncertainty. The weight of unfulfillment felt heavy on my shoulders. My calendar was choc-a-bloc with meetings and presentations. Yet the routine left me yearning for meaning. I held prestigious education degrees and was working a seven-figure salary job. Yet, I felt like a passenger on autopilot, disconnected from my true purpose.

The mirror reflected a tired face, sunken eyes, and slumped shoulders – a stark contrast to the image of success society had painted for me.

I heard a voice from within, urging me to change my career direction. The very next moment, fear gripped me. The corporate career was my identity, and the notion of giving up that identity terrified me. The voice persisted, warning that continuing this path would lead to a perpetual cycle of Monday blues, a life waiting for Fridays.

In a moment of defiance, wiping away my tears, I shouted at the mirror, "No! I want to wake up with a smile every day." And with that declaration, I handed in my notice, defying the skepticism of those around me.

Fast forward to 2021 – a year marked by introspection, self-discovery, and a leap into the unknown. I ventured into the realm of coaching, a field as unfamiliar as it was compelling. I invested in my coach education, actively solicited clients, and engaged in rapid experimentation – often encountering setbacks. It took me many months to realize that beyond being a coach, I had assumed the mantle of an entrepreneur. I started to approach my coaching 'practice' from the lens of a 'business.'

That first year was daunting, with clients scarce and losses overshadowing the topline. Doubts, akin to persistent shadows, permeated my thoughts. Voices inside my head questioned the wisdom of my decision. *Should I give up this nascent initiative and return to the familiar folds of my past?* The recurring question echoed within.

I decided to persevere. Beyond the pursuit of financial gains, my pivot was a personal quest for fulfillment.

Today, as I welcome 2024, the landscape of my life has undergone a profound transformation. I wake up with a smile, not out of obligation but genuine joy. My full client roster spans seven countries, and I proudly hold the recognition of an ICF-accredited PCC Coach. In a little over two and a half years, I have dedicated over 1200 hours to one-on-one client coaching sessions. Once a fledgling endeavor, my coaching business has flourished into a thriving enterprise. In the process, I have earned accolades of being among the Top 10 coaches in Asia and India.

In two years, how did I traverse the path from uncertainty to empowerment, from internal skepticism to international acclaim?

This journey reflects the power of a mindset shift. This story is not just mine; it's a testament to the potential within each of us to craft a life aligned with our dreams.

Part One: The Beginning

I was a shy, introverted child in my formative years. The company of few friends and countless books was my solace. The wisdom of the book *"Rich Dad, Poor Dad,"* laid the foundation of my relationship with money.

I charted an educational course that led me to the prestigious Sri Ram College of Commerce. SRCC remains India's numero uno college for commerce education. One needs to score 95% plus to secure admission. I pursued this milestone with a single-minded focus that brooked no Plan B. And achieved my goal.

My graduation journey commenced with simultaneous preparation for the MBA entrance. I wanted to enter the hallowed halls of the Indian Institute of Management. Three years of self-study paid dividends when I cracked the exam on my first attempt.

Yet, the corridors of SRCC and IIM left me adrift. A gawky, awkward small fish in a big pond, I grappled with an intense sense of impostor syndrome. I believed I lacked social skills and communication prowess.

Somehow, within my inner reservoirs, I unearthed a wellspring of fortitude. I secured a pre-Day Zero campus placement as a management consultant in a Big Four company.

"We like your confidence," they said while extending the offer.

I can put up a good act, I thought, accepting the offer and setting the stage for the next chapter in my narrative.

Part Two: The Messy, and Not-So-Messy, Middle

"How long will it take for the money to get credited to my account?" I asked the teller while handing over my first paycheque. I had taken a lift from a colleague in the middle of the workday to deposit the cheque. The bank branch was three kilometres away from my workplace.

"Is this your first salary?" the cashier asked, sensing my eagerness. The five-figure sum seemed princely to a twenty-two-year-old middle-class girl. I was accustomed to discussing money in four figures till then.

That day marked a pivotal moment in my professional journey. All the hard work seemed worthwhile.

My career advanced, and I kept ascending the corporate ladder. And a lingering sense of 'not belonging' pervaded my mind. I drowned in a sea of MS PowerPoints, delivering presentations for companies worldwide. The corporate landscape buzzed with excitement around expansion and growth strategies. Yet the emphasis on translating these visions into aesthetics began to feel uninspiring.

Looking back, there were silver linings. Three significant aspects were shaping my trajectory for the future. First, I was making money and utilizing it to accumulate a financial cushion. Unwittingly, I was laying the groundwork for a future pivot. Second, I transitioned into a leadership role, guiding and mentoring teams of varied sizes. Third, I was interacting with countless influential stakeholders across several companies. The corporate tenure compelled me to push past my comfort zone, conquer stage fright, and become a public speaker.

I realized I wanted to work more with people than on PowerPoints. The yearning to make a difference in people's lives ushered in the next phase in my journey.

Part Three: The Leap of Faith

In March 2021, after rounds of contemplation and wavering commitments, I bid farewell to my corporate job. It was a calculated risk, propelled by the desire to channel my passion into a profession. With determination superseding planning, I emailed my resignation. My hand trembled as I severed ties with the familiar.

The decision was marked more by certainty about what I didn't want – tied up to the corporate cocoon – than a concrete plan for the way ahead. I was embracing ambiguity by venturing into the field of life and executive coaching. Yes, the allure of money wasn't the driving force. But the absence of a steady income risked knocking my emotions and testing my resilience.

Achieving success in my coaching business wasn't just a goal but a necessity. I wanted to commit to a life aligned with passion and purpose. Like my other goals in the past, there was no Plan B again, for returning to a career I found no joy in was not an option. Making this leap work was the only game that mattered.

Part Four: Manifesting the Business I Wanted

A month later, in April 2021, I painted a vivid picture of the coaching business I aimed to build. Clients, income, systems, working hours and days, vacations – I penned all the details. I then composed a 'Future Letter' to myself – a letter from Smita eighteen months into the future to the present-day me.

This letter was written as if all my business goals had already been achieved. I described a thriving coaching practice with a full client roster (when I had zero clients). I was exceeding monthly income goals within six months of business. My clients enthusiastically referred others to my services. I detailed how I appeared in the media for my work and achieved the ICF PCC certification, which entails 500 client coaching hours. I became a TEDx speaker and built my business website with my own hands in my letter.

Here is what the first five lines of the letter looked like:

"To,

The one who has helped me become successful.

One and a half years ago, I took the plunge to leave the corporate world to set up my coaching practice. It was hard work and took perseverance and dedication. Today, I am happy to see my hard work bear fruit. I have a thriving coaching practice. I have 15 clients a month and coach 4 days a week for 3 weeks a month. I earn INR x,00,000 a month. (This was a six-figure income exceeding my last drawn corporate salary).

I…………….."

This future letter, spanning eight pages, became a cornerstone of my daily routine. I read it aloud, recorded my voice, and listened to it every night for a year. Days were spent tirelessly working toward these goals, while I slept off at night immersed in the description of my dream business. The story in the letter sometimes even invaded my dreams.

A year later, I stopped listening to the voice note. I realized I had accomplished everything detailed in that letter, ahead of schedule. It was time to craft a new future letter, which has become an annual practice.

Part Five: The Present

Today, I have made my mark as an Executive Coach, Personal Empowerment Life Coach, and NLP Practitioner. Holding the prestigious ICF-PCC accreditation, I've dedicated over 1200 hours to one-on-one client coaching in two and a half years.

I specialize in empowering individuals to speak with confidence, get better at what they do, and transform their passion into a profession. My approach resonates with a client base of 250+ individuals across seven countries. The impact of my work echoes in the 100+ client testimonials, affirming the transformative journey we embark on together.

True to my vision, the 'Empower Yourself' coaching practice has grown into a thriving business. My work generates seven-figure revenues and six-figure profitability. A two-time TEDx speaker, I've been honored among the Top 10 Executive Coaches in Asia and India. My ultimate recognition came in September 2023 when the Ministry of Small and Medium Enterprises, Government of India, named me the Best Executive Coach for Professionals and CXOs.

As I revel in following my passion, enjoying the journey, and reaping financial rewards, my story is a testament to the potential within us all. I have not only manifested the career of my dreams once but continue to do so periodically.

My journey is an invitation to you: if I can do this, so can you.

Empower Yourself to Live the Life You Dream: My Blueprint to Cracking the Rich Code

Your journey of transformation begins with the belief that you have the power to shape your destiny.

I've uncovered some crucial principles transcending personal narratives during my professional journey. These aren't mere reflections. They're a roadmap – offering you a pragmatic guide to chart your course, break barriers, and decipher your own rich code. These distilled lessons may empower you in crafting the life you aspire to lead:

1. **Your past does not define your future. You can change the story of your life when and as many times as you want.**
   Shed the constraints of your past. Your history doesn't dictate your destiny. Embrace the power to redefine your narrative. Give yourself the freedom to evolve continuously.

2. **To achieve something, you have to think, act, and feel as if you have already attained it.**

   Visualization is a potent tool when followed by action. Act, think, and feel your goals are already a reality. Prepare and take steps in advance for the life where your dreams have come true. This primes your mind for success and propels you towards your aspirations.

3. **The source of all your achievements is your thoughts. Control your mind to control your life.**

   Master your thoughts, and you master your destiny. Understand the influence of your mind on your actions and be careful of what you think about. Positive, focused thoughts fuel constructive actions and outcomes.

4. **Consistency and discipline have a far more significant role to play in success than talent. Talent can be developed with time, but you must work to achieve consistency.**

   Talent is a starting point, not the finish line. The consistent, disciplined effort is the backbone of lasting success. Cultivate habits that align with your goals and stick to them.

5. **You have to stay invested in the process to achieve the results. You must also know what you want to attain to build a process around it.**

   Results are born from a commitment to the journey. You also risk getting lost in the undertaking without knowing what path to take. Clearly define your goals, then build and refine your process.

   Be adaptable but stay committed to the process. Results are a natural by-product of a robust approach.

6. **You need to create your own definition of success to be truly successful. Borrowed or imitated success is a failure.**

Avoid the pitfalls of comparison; everyone's path is unique. I would have felt far more overwhelmed – and will still do – if I started comparing my business to another coach's. That will be like comparing apples to oranges; you can only eat one at a time.

Your goals, values, and aspirations shape your journey. Define success on your terms. Authentic success comes from aligning your actions with your personal vision.

7. **Fail fast, fail often, but try to avoid falling hard – that's the essence of building a successful business.**
Embrace failures as stepping stones. Success is one of the ten things that works.

Quick, small failures are lessons learned. Navigate through them, and success becomes a series of stepping stones rather than a distant summit.

8. **Think and dream big, but act on one small thing at a time.**
Ambitious dreams need practical steps. Chunk down grand visions into manageable tasks and focus on the next small activity. Consistent small actions accumulate into monumental achievements.

9. **Keep an eye on numbers. But your business should stand for something beyond numbers to be successful.**
Who are you serving? Who do you want to help?

Metrics are crucial, but the heartbeat of your business is its purpose. Define your mission and understand your audience. Measure success not in profits but in impact.

10. **You must desire something badly to get it. Your Plan B for success should be not to have a Plan B.**

Unyielding desire fuels determination. Commit wholeheartedly; eliminate retreat as an option. A relentless pursuit of your goals creates the conditions for success.

Not getting rich shouldn't be a choice if you want to get rich.

11. **A successful Career/Business is where Passion Meets Purpose to Create a Profession that generates Profit. Nothing in this equation is exclusive.**

Forge a career aligned with your passion and purpose. The convergence of these elements lays the foundation for a fulfilling and prosperous profession.

Passion sustains you through the challenges, ensuring longevity in your chosen field. Purpose adds depth to your pursuits, infusing meaning into monetary gains. Without passion, the journey becomes arduous, lacking the fuel to endure. The absence of purpose diminishes the allure of profit, leaving you without the conviction needed to navigate the lows with resilience and determination.

Each of the four aspects complements the others in the journey toward success.

Act on these principles. Create the career you love, find time for everything you like, and live your dream life. Empower Yourself to Crack the Rich Code.

The Last Word: Destiny is Not Chance but Choice

"You hold the pen to script your destiny; dare to write a story that echoes with the thunder of your potential."

- *Smita Das Jain*

In the grand tapestry of life, your potential is woven from the threads of your thoughts, actions, and determination. The triumphs, struggles, and eventual success are not exclusive to any one individual. I am as human as you – you can emulate and even exceed my achievements. The power to transform your life lies within your grasp.

Let my story be a call to you to reclaim your narrative.

Success begins with a resolute mindset. Act as if you've already achieved your goals, and watch the world align with your aspirations.

If self-doubt, fear, or apprehension clouds your path, know this: you are not alone. Help me extend a helping hand to guide you through the fog of uncertainties. Book an Empower Yourself Strategy Session with me at https://www.lifecoachsmitadjain.com/booking. Let's chart a course for your success together. Whether it's building confidence, overcoming challenges, or defining your own version of success, I am here to assist.

Empower yourself. Let nothing and no one – including you and your own hesitations – stand between you and your goals.

Your success is not just a possibility; it's an inevitability waiting to be embraced.

***

To contact Smita:

Website: https://www.lifecoachsmitadjain.com/

Email: smitadjain@lifecoachsmitadjain.com

Phone: +91 997 112 0553

Schedule a Strategy Session: https://www.lifecoachsmitadjain.com/booking

LinkedIn: https://www.linkedin.com/in/smitadasjain/

Instagram: https://www.instagram.com/smitadjain/

David Radosevich, Ph.D.

David Radosevich, Ph.D. is a psychologist focused on peak performance, leadership, and team culture. His purpose is to coach the mindset and skills people need to achieve what's possible in their lives. He practices his craft as an executive consultant to C-suite leaders of Fortune 500 companies, as a professor who teaches students how to distinguish themselves in business, and as a performance coach who trains elite athletes to raise the bar on their leadership, teamwork, and emotional intelligence. The common thread is empowering people to develop the mindset to be their very best. David is a published, peer-reviewed author with an international best-selling book and a speaker on helping people elevate their game and accelerate their impact.

For over two decades, David has been helping organizations develop and maximize their human capital to drive business success, using business tools such as executive assessment, selection, training, needs assessment, and performance management. His clients have included Meta, Wal-Mart, Schering Plough, the New York State Police, and Developmental Dimensions International, where he has assessed thousands of leaders from hundreds of Fortune 500 firms.

Dr. Radosevich lectures regularly on the fusion of business and psychology to drive peak performance in the workforce. David's current project is delivering high-value peak performance training and writing a book to help people apply neuroscientific tools to their professional and personal lives.

Neuro-Leverage: Your Brain's Unstoppable Formula for Success

Dr. David Radosevich

The Pain Points

"It's not the load that breaks you down; it's the way you carry it."

- Lou Holtz

During our first coaching session, Victoria expressed her struggles as a CEO, "Starting this business as the founder was much easier than growing it. The honeymoon is over, and I'm unsure I can take the team and the business to the next level."

When I asked what issues keep her up most at night, Victoria confessed, "I am putting out fires daily! Our communication and focus is off. People have burnout by being connected 24/7. Several strategic decisions have backed us into a corner with bottlenecks. Frankly, the only hint of innovation is that motivational poster hanging in the lobby."

As I thought about the complexity she faced as her industry was affected by technology's rapid change and uncertainty, I asked curiously, "How much time do you dedicate to off-the-grid deep thinking to get ahead of changes coming at you?" Victoria said, "We have bi-annual strategy sessions, but I am too distracted with the day-to-day operations to dedicate more time."

Victoria's resigned look was palpable as if she realized the inadequacy of her answer. "I pride myself on doing it all. I try to be a great mom and wife. I want to scale this business while staying healthy. But honestly, every time we plug one hole in our sinking boat, two more pop up. It's nonstop! What does that say about me as a leader?" she questioned in desperation.

When I asked how she shows up for her family and herself, Victoria described in a trailing voice, "I get home in time to tuck my kids in bed, but it isn't the quality time they deserve. I could be in better shape and eat fewer meals at my desk. I am always exhausted and lost my resiliency."

I then asked Victoria, "What would it mean to you if you could design your life differently by using your biology for you instead of against you?" Victoria excitedly jumped in, "You mean there is a better way than this madness?"

"Definitely! For years, you have trained your craft. The diplomas on your wall and ongoing training have gotten you to this point. However, you need to train your mind to amplify your effectiveness," I explained. "Elite athletes, special forces, and top executives have had access to the best brain science and peak performance training. Why can't you do it too?"

Victoria was all in, "Well, if there is a formula for leveraging my mind to build a stronger organization, then I am all in!"

I reassured her, "I love the fire! Successful leaders are willing to do the work necessary to live better. Let's dive in by me first telling you about how a mouse can lift an elephant."

Can A Mouse Lift An Elephant?

> *"Give me a lever long enough and a fulcrum on which to place it, and I shall move the world."*
>
> *- Archimedes*

Ann Tompert's children's story *"Just a Little Bit"* teaches us that innovative thinking can help a mouse lift an elephant. We can use this metaphor to illustrate the power of using neuroscience as leverage.

Imagine the elephant is the workload and the mouse is the effort needed to move it. Using a crowbar without a fulcrum is nearly impossible. However, using the crowbar with a fulcrum, the elephant can be moved with less effort simply by moving the fulcrum closer to it.

Neurochemistry is the Fulcrum

What is the fulcrum that we can use in our lives? It is our biology and neurochemistry. When we assume that the fulcrum can shift either towards or away from the heavy workload, the burning question becomes how can we consistently move the fulcrum closer to the elephant to make the mouse's job easier?

Although the application of neuroscience to business is in its infancy, research continually provides more clarity on how to solve pressing business issues. Some key findings focus on how leverage releases dopamine and norepinephrine, which helps us stay focused and driven to accomplish our goals.

Another benefit of leverage involves lowering cognitive load. As our brain becomes overwhelmed, thinking clearly and making effective decisions becomes challenging. By implementing systems, automating processes, and delegating tasks, we can free up mental resources and reduce cognitive load, allowing our brains to function more efficiently.

Third, leveraging mental frameworks to organize and understand complex information allows our brains to process info quickly. Finally, when we consistently use leverage, our brains rewire neural pathways that support our future leveraged behaviors.

Understanding the neuroscience behind leverage can optimize our brain's functioning and enhance our productivity. Leveraging our brains' natural processes allows us to work smarter and achieve more extraordinary results with less stress.

Ultimately, the premise of this chapter involves learning how to use your biology for you instead of against you to drive success. Combining brain science with a savvy use of leverage, I am introducing the concept that I term "neuro-leverage." Neuro-leverage helps leaders transform how they make strategic decisions, build high-performing teams, innovate, and excel in other critical leadership imperatives.

Circling back to Victoria's pain points, the following sections will offer a brief overview of how she can enhance her leadership effectiveness in the critical areas she highlighted.

Neuro-Leverage Your Turbulence

> *"When everything seems to be going against you, remember that the airplane takes off against the wind, not with it."*
>
> *- Henry Ford*

Leading oneself, a high-performing team, or an elite organization is difficult. Our current environment is characterized by volatility, uncertainty, complexity, and ambiguity, which comprise a turbulent state called VUCA. The

U.S. Army War College coined this term after the Cold War to describe the rapidly changing battlefields. The business world has since adopted this term to describe the challenges in professional and personal domains.

Most leaders, like Victoria, struggle with turbulent work and home environments, but few are equipped to handle them, leading to personal, professional, and physical struggles. The good news, however, is that we can use turbulence to our advantage if we understand how it impacts our biology. Essentially, turbulence triggers specific reactions in our brain and nervous system. Our brain perceives it as a potential threat, leading to stress hormone release, which causes increased arousal and alertness in the short term.

Arousal is key, as it operates under the Goldilocks principle. Too little arousal leads to apathy or boredom, and too much arousal leads to anxiety. However, just the right amount of arousal can help us enter a flow state where we feel our best and perform our best.

Peak performers rise to the challenge of turbulence through awareness of how their body is responding physically and then taking targeted actions. One strategy involves shifting arousal levels up or down depending on the situation to ensure the optimal amount needed for effective performance. Standard techniques include breathwork, regular exercise, or some form of calming the mind to reset levels of focus.

Second, separating turbulence across different life domains helps balance our arousal levels. For instance, a wise strategy for those in a fast-paced, high-stress job would be to ensure that their personal life is calm and predictable. Alternatively, a more adventurous or complex hobby could balance a mundane job.

Third, to perform at peak levels during high turbulence, researchers suggest flow triggers like clear goals, feedback, concentration, autonomy, risk, and curiosity. Setting goals that challenge us but not to the point of breaking is vital. By optimizing this challenge-skills ratio, we can regulate the proper level of arousal in the nervous system to show up at our best.

The goal is to flip the script on turbulence and use it as an advantage to drive growth and innovation. Specifically, we can use neuroscience to turn volatility into vision, uncertainty into certainty, complexity into simplicity, and ambiguity into clarity. We can design our environment around us rather than simply being at the mercy of it.

In Victoria's case, she could neuro-leverage:

- Volatility: Develop an adaptive mindset to guide the team with a clear vision and calibrate priorities in real-time.

- Uncertainty: Anticipate and address the most pressing bottleneck to create change.

- Complexity: Create a culture of agile learners and ensure systems are in place for the team to regulate arousal levels to prevent the nervous system from being overwhelmed.

- Ambiguity: Impeccably clarify messages to align the team's needs and motives with critical business goals.

Neuro-Leverage Your People

"Individually, we are one drop. Together, we are an ocean." - Ryunosuke Satoro

Effective leadership is a game of social dynamics that builds authentic relationships. Social identity theory, developed in the 1970s, reveals that social groups can form distinctive identities that may lead to favoritism or conflicts. Proactively managing these dynamics can foster a more inclusive, innovative, and collaborative business culture.

Modern scientists like Michael Platt at the University of Pennsylvania have built on this foundational research, describing how leaders must develop their social brains. He states that the different structural areas of the brain and the neural wiring impact humans' ability to form social connections. Recent research done at Dartmouth by Uri Hasson and Thalia Wheatley suggests that people's brains can adapt to each other during conversation, creating a "super brain" effect that amplifies collective brain activity.

Another fascinating study by Norihhiro Sadato showed that eye contact for two minutes before a high school class prepared the social brain to synchronize with others' intentions and actions. Leaders can use storytelling, fun games, or mirroring language to prepare teams for brain synchronization before meetings or work blocks. Chris Voss's book "Never Split The Difference" highlights the impact of mirroring. As a former FBI hostage negotiator, he used mirroring techniques to build rapport, gain information, and encourage productive communication. Voss had an impressive track record of achieving peaceful resolutions during high-stakes negotiations.

Leadership styles have a significant impact on neuro-leveraging others. Richard Boyatzis found that authoritarian approaches shut down openness and perspective-taking, while consensus-based leadership fosters a more effective work environment. Typical delegation can be prescriptive and highlight power dynamics. Conversely, true empowerment creates a more engaging work environment with the proper guidance for success that allows people the latitude to make decisions.

Empowerment is a potent source of neuro-leverage. Dopamine is a critical player in motivation and reward and can be triggered when we empower tasks to others and envision successful completion. Norepinephrine helps maintain attentiveness during the delegation process. Serotonin is called the "feel-good" chemical and provides a sense of accomplishment through empowering delegations. Oxytocin, the "trust hormone," promotes connection and collaboration when projects are handed off.

What does this mean for business success? Neurochemical responses vary greatly depending on individuals and contexts. However, understanding these responses can give valuable insights into delegation processes. Leaders must align their team's neural activity to maximize productivity and foster strong relationships.

In Victoria's case, she could neuro-leverage:

- In-group vs. out-group: Ensure everyone knows they belong by genuinely connecting.

- Physical synchrony: Build trust through eye contact, mirroring others' words and tone, and taking breaks to reset the brain when it is strained at a neurochemical level.

- Power differences: Downplay hierarchy and power to encourage openness by sending clear invitations of empowerment rather than directive delegations.

- Perspective-taking and emotional intelligence: Focus on commonalities and others' needs to promote emotional intelligence as a driver of team chemistry.

Neuro-Leverage Your Innovation

"Innovation is the calling card of the future."

- Anna Eshoo

Innovation is critical to the success and longevity of any business. To foster a culture of innovation, influential leaders motivate employees to generate novel and valuable ideas that add measurable value to the customers. Such a culture encourages employees to question conventional thinking, take calculated risks, and seize new opportunities to tackle current challenges. However, many leaders overestimate their organizations' innovation effectiveness without seeking regular feedback from objective experts outside their business who can provide additional perspective.

As Victoria's example shows, when urgent operational issues arise, innovation often takes a backseat. Consequently, organizations gradually lose their innovative edge and fail to create unique solutions to give them a competitive advantage.

Organizations can approach innovation like MacGyver or MacGruber, two fictional TV characters with vastly different approaches. The iconic MacGyver uses creativity and resourcefulness to solve problems, while MacGruber is impulsive and often fails. The key for organizations is to leverage the mind's natural processes for better creativity.

Our understanding of innovation has evolved as we uncover the secrets of the mind. For instance, the traditional belief in the left-brain/right-brain dichotomy has been replaced with the concept of two modes of operation in the brain that activate both hemispheres.

The brain can be compared to a car engine with drive or park modes. When our brain is in drive mode, it functions like an active engine, propelling us forward with focus and optimal performance. Neuroscientists call this mode the "frontoparietal attention network," which is essential in attentional control and executive functioning. By filtering out distractions, it helps us focus on critical tasks that need our attention. Therefore, just like how we put our cars in drive mode to move forward, we need to shift our brains into drive mode to gain momentum with our goals.

When the brain is in park mode, it's like idling your car in a rest area with a beautiful view. It's a state of mental rest that allows the brain to engage in daydreaming, introspection, and mind-wandering, which are required for creating new ideas. When you park your car at a rest area, you can switch drivers, grab a snack, rest your eyes, or determine a new route. Similarly, innovation also requires the brain to calm down. Neuroscientists refer to this parking mode as the "default mode network." It helps us process social information and generate innovative breakthroughs.

It's important to understand that, like vehicles, our brains can't simultaneously be in park and drive modes. When it comes to innovation, intentionally shifting our high cognitive energy work from drive mode to park mode becomes necessary. Being in park mode allows us to utilize the neurochemicals required to create an ideal state of mind for innovation.

At the neurochemical level, serotonin and endorphins help create a positive emotional state that supports creative thinking, while dopamine and norepinephrine enhance our focus and pattern recognition. On the other hand, oxytocin promotes social bonding and collaboration, which can be beneficial in generating innovative ideas in group settings. Individuals and organizations can utilize knowledge of neurochemicals to foster creativity, collaboration, and idea generation.

Leaders play a vital role in promoting innovation within their organizations. A culture that trains employees, provides autonomy, and empowers them to take calculated risks is necessary for fostering innovation. Encouraging collaboration among employees can lead to the exchange of creative ideas. Embracing experimentation and failure can provide security and encourage people to explore new, bold ideas. Providing resources and support can help individuals overcome obstacles and transform their ideas into reality.

To promote creative thinking, try engaging in activities such as playing exploration games or walking. Taking cold showers, practicing meditation, and scheduling innovation time based on your optimal brain state can also help enhance creativity.

In Victoria's case, she could neuro-leverage:

- Drive vs. park modes: Engage the default mode network to maximize creativity.

- Foster an innovative culture: Encourage curiosity by asking thought-provoking questions and supporting experimentation.

- Calm the mind: Engage in exploration games, walks, and other stress-reducing activities.

- Chronotype alignment: Ensure that people do their creative thinking at the time of day that aligns best with their energy patterns.

The Clear Path Forward

"Every system is perfectly designed to get the results it gets."

W. Edwards Deming

As Victoria's coaching session was coming to an end, I asked her to reflect on the significant insights that resonated with her. She replied, "First, I need to read the owner's manual for my brain. I have not been using it correctly to make myself feel and perform better. Second, I need to go to the hardware store to purchase their largest crowbar and fulcrum!" she laughed.

During our conversation, we emphasized the significance of creating a new approach to working, leading, and living. The key to achieving this is developing a framework that considers the most fundamental aspect of every human being - our biology. We cannot outsmart the way our biological system is designed to function. Attempting to take shortcuts or manipulate the system will only result in reduced creativity, increased burnout, and overall ineffectiveness in the long term.

As advances in neuroscience are being applied in business, the potential to make significant strides is timely as the exponential rate of change presents more challenges and opportunities. Those leaders who channel their inner MacGyver by using their neurochemical fulcrum to their advantage will be the proverbial mouse who can lift an elephant.

On the other hand, leaders who refuse to put their brains in park mode and insist on constantly pushing forward with an execution-only mindset risk missing out on valuable opportunities for innovation that could help transform their businesses and set them apart from the competition. Therefore, it is essential for leaders to be open to new ideas and strategies from neuroscience and to be willing to take a step back and evaluate their current approach to achieve exponential long-term success.

Further, it's important to note that this is merely the beginning of a broader spectrum of neuro-leverage sources. While competently managing unstable situations, empowering individuals, and fostering innovation are undeniably critical aspects of a successful business, numerous other sources of leverage must be fully comprehended and incorporated into an efficient system to achieve the desired outcomes.

As I concluded my conversation with Victoria, I expressed my sincere hopes for our ongoing coaching partnership, "My goal is to assist you in finding joy in pursuing your personal and professional aspirations. Integrating neuroscience into your business practices can improve your leadership skills, create exceptional teams, and foster innovation. Neuro-leverage is the unstoppable formula for success."

***

To contact David:

LinkedIn: https://www.linkedin.com/in/davidradosevich/

Website: https://successence.net/

Email: david@successence.net

Julie Hruska

Julie Hruska is a High Performance Coach, Strategist, and Trainer. With a master's degree in education and an advanced coaching certification from the prestigious High Performance Institute, as well over 2500 hours of training in yoga, meditation, and mindfulness, Julie has helped countless individuals and organizations achieve unprecedented success.

As the founder of Powerful Leaders LLC, Julie's mission is to awaken, empower, and inspire people to become the best versions of themselves. She specializes in guiding clients to perform at their optimal levels by mastering their mindset, up-leveling their skill sets, and developing high-performance habits across all areas of life.

Julie's expertise empowers individuals and executive teams to break through any obstacles, preventing them from achieving success. Beyond her work with individuals, Julie is a sought-after trainer who has worked with top executives and companies to develop high-performance cultures that lead to increased engagement, optimized performance, and revenue growth.

Julie resides in the beautiful mountains of Western North Carolina with her youngest son and her spirited Shiba Inu. Julie's two older children are college-aged and are discovering their way in the world. In addition to coaching and parenting, Julie is an avid traveler with a love for international explorations. When she's not working or traveling, you'll find Julie on long walks with her dog, practicing pilates, or eating at a delicious farm-to-table restaurant. Julie lives each day to the fullest and encourages others to do the same. She lives by the motto, "You only live once, but if you do it right, once is enough" and encourages you to do the same.

"Generating Wealth: Transforming Limiting Beliefs by Cultivating an Abundance Mindset"

By Julie Hruska

When it comes to creating financial freedom, the role of mindset cannot be overstated. Before embarking on your wealth generation journey, you must work through your antiquated views about money. The secrets to financial success begin with your thoughts. Unraveling the layers of psychological patterns that influence your financial behavior is essential. Once you understand those patterns, you can cultivate an unshakable abundance mindset that transcends your limiting beliefs and shift from the confines of scarcity to the boundless realm of opportunity and expansion!

As you unlock the doors to a world of unparalleled growth and prosperity and learn to harness the power of an abundance mindset, you will gain a heightened sense of confidence, impeccable decision-making skills, and an increased likelihood of amassing wealth at an accelerated pace.

My Story

I grew up in a conservative Christian family where my dad handled the finances. He was a good provider and always ensured we had what we needed, but he didn't splurge often. I went to school in a wealthy district and often saw people who had more than me. I didn't want to wear hand-me-downs and make hard choices with money, so I imagined an abundant life filled with ease. I married young and following my parent's model, let my husband, at the time, manage our finances because that fit traditional gender roles. We had a nice upper-middle-class lifestyle, but after our divorce, I was thrust into financial ruin. Months without child support on a teacher's salary supporting four people and lawyer's fees put us in a difficult position. Suddenly moving from a supplemental income to being the sole provider proved treacherous because I had never run a household and had limited experience managing finances. Juggling two jobs, a house, and finances while raising three kids on my own with a teaching salary was a tremendous challenge. Add that to my desire for an abundant lifestyle without the income to match it, and we had the ultimate recipe for disaster. I cycled in and out of debt, trying to provide my kids and myself with the life I'd envisioned. It seemed like a vicious cycle of lack and abundance for years. Fortunately, I learned to transform my mindset, gained financial literacy, and became very disciplined with my finances. I did what I needed to do to break the cycle, freeing us from a life of scarcity. Now, we are living more abundantly, and I am working toward generating true wealth in our lives. I chose to write this guide for you because of my experiences and the challenges some of my clients have related to their scarcity mindsets. I pray it serves you well so you can cultivate an abundance mindset, experience financial freedom, and live your best life.

Understanding Your Money Mindset

Before diving into the strategies necessary for cultivating an abundance mindset, it is essential to understand the concept of a scarcity mindset and its pervasive influence on your financial decision-making. A scarcity mindset is characterized by a belief in limited resources, a constant fear of lack, and a focus on what is missing rather than what is possible. People trapped in a scarcity mindset often approach financial matters with anxiety, viewing money as a finite resource and wealth as unattainable. They also find themselves trapped in a cycle of worry, self-doubt, and a constant preoccupation with financial limitations.

When you have a scarcity mindset, you fear risk-taking and hold yourself back in many ways. You don't live your best life because you aren't free to. You're held captive by your thoughts. The impact of a scarcity mindset is far-reaching, affecting your financial decisions and overall well-being. Chronic stress, fear of failure, and a tendency to make impulsive decisions are common expressions of a scarcity mindset. Breaking free from the confines of scarcity requires a conscious effort to rewire ingrained thought patterns and replace them with beliefs that foster abundance. Take time now to list your money-related fears and anxieties as we shift toward creating an abundance mindset.

_____

_____

_____

_____

_____

_____

_____

_____

The journey to develop an abundance mindset begins by reflecting on your relationship with money. Let's take the time to do so now. Take a moment to contemplate and journal about the following questions:

What attitudes, beliefs, and emotions do I have surrounding money?

_____

_____

_____

_____

What does money represent to me?

_____

_____

_____

_____

How do I feel when I think about budgeting, saving, or investing?

_____

_____

_____

_____

This exercise will provide valuable insights into your financial mindset and help you identify any unconscious patterns or biases influencing your financial decisions.

Influences On Your Money Mindset

Scarcity beliefs often originate from early life experiences, cultural influences, or societal expectations. A significant factor in the way we view money comes from our childhood. Our early experiences and observations, particularly within the family context, often significantly shape our financial behaviors. Your parents' money patterns shape your subconscious beliefs about money. Here are three examples from my high-performance clients that show how our early life environment and parents' beliefs often become our own:

Tim grew up bouncing from house to house and was even homeless for brief periods of time. His experiences created patterns of binging and hoarding due to a lack of food and shelter. His basic needs were not consistently met, undermining his sense of safety and security. When he became wealthy, he struggled with overspending to compensate for his feelings of inadequacy growing up as a "poor kid." These early experiences with financial instability deeply ingrained fear of scarcity in Tim, leading him to equate large quantities of food and material possessions with abundance and to equate wealth with security and self-worth. As an adult, his past traumas manifested in the relentless pursuit of material possessions, attempting to fill the emotional voids of his childhood and prove his worth to himself and others. He struggled with his weight as he overate due to food insecurity as a child. By identifying and working through his scarcity mindset, Tim overcame these issues and created abundance in all areas of his life.

Jack grew up in a wealthy family. His parents spent recklessly and gave him whatever he wanted. He took money for granted and struggled with overspending as an adult because he didn't have the financial literacy to budget effectively and had unrealistic views related to the ease of wealth generation. He wasn't earning the money necessary to sustain the lifestyle he was raised in and had to reset his relationship with money as well. Jack's upbringing in a financially abundant environment led him to develop a sense of entitlement and a lack of appreciation for the value of money. This disconnect resulted in poor financial decision-making as an adult, as he was ill-prepared for the realities of managing and earning money independently. His journey towards financial stability required a fundamental shift in his understanding of money, learning to differentiate between needs and wants, and developing the discipline to live within his means.

Allison grew up with very frugal parents. They pinched every penny and sometimes lacked the resources to pay for the extra things other children had. As an adult, she worked hard and earned a mid-6 figure income; however, she had high-stress levels about money. Her scarcity mindset prevented her from enjoying some of her favorite pleasures, such as high-end spas, Michelin star dinners, and international vacations. Her scarcity mindset was a significant detriment to her happiness. Even though she had the means to enjoy her wealth, she had to shift her mindset.

As you can see from these examples, our parents' relationships with money often become our own without us even realizing it. These beliefs are deeply ingrained and can manifest in many ways. The good news is that you can redefine your relationship with money. It's important to reflect on your parents' attitudes towards spending, saving, and investing and any messages or values they conveyed about money. Understanding the financial dynamics within your family can help you recognize patterns that you have inherited and provide a foundation for making intentional changes as needed. Take time to journal about your parents' relationship with money and how it has impacted your views.

_____

_____

_____

_____

_____

_____

_____

_____

_____

Now determine which views you'd like to change.

_____

_____

_____

_____

It's important to approach this exploration with curiosity and empathy, never judging your parents. Their parents likely influenced them regarding money, just as you were, and they passed those beliefs down to you without even realizing it. Trust that your parents were doing what they thought was best as the time and work rewrite your antiquated views on money. Understanding the influences that shaped your financial mindset will empower you to make more informed and conscious financial decisions.

Cultivating Mindfulness and Awareness

The first step towards cultivating an abundance mindset is developing mindfulness and awareness, which the exercises you've just completed were helping you do. Mindfulness involves being fully present in the moment and acknowledging your thoughts and emotions without judgment. Practicing mindfulness creates space to observe your financial beliefs and behaviors objectively. Here are some additional questions to contemplate and journal about:

Are your views related to money predominantly positive or negative?

_____

What financial limitations do you find yourself dwelling on?

_____

_____

Your responses will help you identify your scarcity triggers and consciously redirect your focus towards abundance.

The Psychological Impact of a Scarcity Mindset

In the realm of psychological well-being, few areas are as pervasive and impactful as your beliefs about money. Scarcity beliefs, rooted in the fear of not having enough, can significantly influence your thoughts, emotions, and behaviors. Scarcity beliefs about money can lead to a range of negative psychological outcomes, including heightened stress, anxiety, and a diminished sense of self-worth. Individuals may adopt defensive financial behaviors such as excessive saving, reluctance to invest, or an inability to enjoy present moments due to the fear of an uncertain future. Recognizing the psychological toll that scarcity beliefs can take on overall well-being is essential. Both personally and professionally, in my role as a high-performance coach, I have witnessed the transformative power of reframing scarcity beliefs into an abundant perspective.

Moving From Scarcity to Abundance

To lessen the impact of scarcity beliefs on your life, you must learn to reframe these beliefs and cultivate a more abundant mindset. To do so, you must identify your scarcity beliefs, challenge their validity, and replace them with more abundant ones. Even though this sounds simple, what is happening internally is actually quite complex. Reframing scarcity beliefs to abundant beliefs is a neurological process. Neuroplasticity and cognitive restructuring are required to reset your default mode. Neuroplasticity, your brain's ability to reorganize itself, occurs when you consciously engage in reframing your beliefs. When you engage in this practice, your brain builds new neural pathways. Those pathways are strengthened when you reframe a scarcity belief to an abundant one. Reframing beliefs involves cognitive restructuring, which is the process of changing your thought patterns. When you consistently challenge and alter your old patterns, changes in neural pathways associated with perceiving and interpreting situations occur. All of which lead to our ultimate goal of resetting your default mode. Your default mode, formally known as your Default Mode Network (DMN), is a network of your brain regions that are active when your mind is at rest (aka your subconscious). When your default mode becomes one of abundance rather than scarcity, you have a more positive and constructive internal narrative. And that's the game changer.

Here is how you reset your default mode. It's a process of consistently identifying, challenging and reframing your thoughts until it's habitual. For example, if you believe "I never have enough money." Ask yourself, "Is this true?" Once you recognize the lie, tell yourself, "That is not true. I have enough money to cover my expenses now and am open to attracting more abundance in my life."

Now it's your turn to try. List three scarcity beliefs below. Confront the validity of each, then write a more affirming, abundant thought to replace your scarce belief with.

1. Scarcity Belief:

   _____
   _____

   Confrontation:

   _____
   _____

   Abundant Thought:

   _____
   _____

2. Scarcity Belief:

   _____
   _____

   Confrontation:

   _____
   _____

   Abundant Thought:

   _____
   _____

3. Scarcity Belief:

   _____
   _____

   Confrontation:

   _____
   _____

   Abundant Thought:

   _____
   _____

Transforming scarcity beliefs into abundant perspectives is a gradual and empowering process. It takes consistent practice to shift from scarcity to abundance. Over time, you will shift your default mode and possess an abundant mindset. As reframing becomes a habit, it will be less cumbersome, and eventually, you won't even have to think about it. Abundance will be a part of who you are. Developing a healthier relationship with money that promotes resilience, self-efficacy, and a sense of abundance is critical to creating wealth and living a fulfilling life. By implementing these strategies, you can break free from the constraints of scarcity thinking and embrace a mindset that opens the door to financial well-being and overall life satisfaction.

Generating Gratitude

In addition to being mindful, gratitude is a critical component of an abundance mindset.

Begin each day by expressing gratitude for the financial aspects of your life, regardless of their scale. Focus on times of financial success, no matter how small. This practice trains your mind to appreciate the existing abundance and fosters a positive outlook for your financial journey. By focusing on the positives, you gradually rewire your brain to seek abundance rather than scarcity.

The language we use internally and externally significantly influences our mindset. Affirmations and positive self-talk are potent tools for reshaping your beliefs about money. Create a list of empowering financial affirmations tailored to your goals and aspirations. Repeat these affirmations daily to reinforce a positive and abundant mindset. For example:

"I am a magnet for financial prosperity."

"I am so happy that money consistently comes to me in increasing quantities through multiple sources."

"I attract abundance in all areas of my life."

By consistently incorporating affirming language into your thoughts and conversations, you create a mental environment conducive to abundance.

The Power of Visualization

Visualization is another powerful technique to create an abundance mindset. Take time each day to visualize your financial success vividly. Picture yourself achieving your financial goals and living your best life, experiencing the emotions associated with that success. Create a clear vision of your ideal financial future, including details such as a comfortable lifestyle, financial freedom, and philanthropic endeavors. Visualize how financial abundance will add to the quality of your life and the lives of the people you care about. The more vivid and emotionally charged your visualizations are, the more effectively they will contribute to reshaping your mindset. Visualization not only reinforces positive beliefs but also helps you align your actions with your aspirations. Visualization provides a foundation to build upon.

Growth and Abundance

A growth mindset, as coined by psychologist Carol Dweck, is the belief that abilities and intelligence can be developed through dedication and hard work. When applied to finances, a growth mindset indicates that your financial situation is not fixed but can be changed with consistent effort. Challenge yourself to view your financial difficulties and setbacks as opportunities for growth rather than insurmountable obstacles. Embrace setbacks as learning experiences and adjust your financial strategies accordingly. Adopting a growth mindset empowers you to overcome challenges and continually progress toward financial abundance.

Surrounding Yourself with Success

As you discovered earlier about how your parents influenced your relationship with money, the people and environments you expose yourself to play a crucial role in shaping your financial mindset. Evaluating your social circle and seeking individuals who inspire positivity and abundance is essential. Additionally, engaging in conversations that uplift and encourage rather than perpetuate scarcity-driven narratives is crucial. Attending events, joining communities, or participating in forums focusing on financial empowerment and success is also beneficial. To deepen your experiences and get a taste of the life you desire, consider surrounding yourself with luxury and high-net-worth individuals. Eat at fine dining restaurants, buy first-class tickets, and stay at luxury hotels when possible. This gives you a taste of the lifestyle you are working toward. By immersing yourself in an environment that fosters abundance, you engage in higher-level conversations and reinforce your commitment to cultivating an abundance mindset aligned with prosperity.

As a caveat, while surrounding yourself with success gives you a taste of the lifestyle you are working toward, only do so when you have the available resources. Beyond an occasional splurge, though, live below your means, save, and invest well. The one thing I've learned through my journey as a single mother of three, from lack to abundance, is that you can't work your way into wealth; you must invest. Knowing how, when, and where to save and invest is part of the financial literacy you must develop to shift from thinking about abundance to generating it.

Developing Financial Literacy

In addition to developing your mindset, you must develop your skill set to generate wealth. Knowledge is a powerful antidote to fear and uncertainty. Take proactive steps to enhance your financial literacy by educating yourself on various aspects of personal finance. Learn about budgeting, saving, and investing, and stay informed about economic trends. The more knowledgeable you are about financial matters, the more empowered you will feel in making informed decisions. This empowerment is a cornerstone of an abundance mindset, as it shifts your perspective from a passive observer to an active participant in your financial journey.

From Theory to Practice

In unveiling the ultimate strategies for cultivating an unshakable abundance mindset, we've explored the transformative power of mindfulness, gratitude, affirmations, visualization, a growth mindset, positive environments, and financial education. This holistic approach not only enhances our mental and emotional well-being but also sets a strong foundation for achieving lasting prosperity. The journey from scarcity to abundance is a process that requires consistent effort and a commitment to reshaping ingrained thought patterns. I encourage you to embark on this journey with an open mind and a willingness to embrace change. By incorporating these strategies into your daily life, you will shift your mindset and lay the foundation for sustained financial abundance, which leads to greater levels of happiness and resilience and a profound sense of empowerment in your personal and financial life. Remember, the boundless realm of opportunity and expansion awaits those who dare to cultivate an abundance mindset and embrace the limitless possibilities to generate wealth.

Based on the information shared in this chapter, my key takeaways include:

_____

_____

_____

_____

_____

_____

_____

_____

Changes I commit to making are:

_____

_____

_____

_____

_____

_____

_____

_____

_____

_____

***

To contact Julie:

Julie@powerfulleaders.com

https://www.powerfulleaders.com/

https://www.linkedin.com/in/julie-hruska/

Baz Porter

After hitting rock bottom from childhood trauma and addiction, Baz Porter had a monumental realization - his pain prepared him to guide others out of the darkness. This epiphany set Baz on a path of radical personal transformation that led him to become an empowering life coach.

Baz now facilitates holistic growth in clients by integrating personal development, mindfulness, and strategic planning. His approach centers on living purposefully from the heart. Baz created a 4-part framework called R.A.M.S to coach individuals comprehensively on achieving sustainable success.

By embracing his past, Baz transformed trauma into a gift for relating to others' struggles with empathy. He passionately serves people ready to rewrite their stories and reclaim their power. Nothing brings Baz greater joy than playing a role in someone's breakthrough.

Baz finds fulfillment in spreading ripples of hope through his community. In helping others transform, he sees the positive effects in his own life. Baz feels humbled by each soul willing to let him walk with them on their journey.

If Baz's story resonates, he encourages you to meet him for coffee and a life-changing chat about your vision. You can align with your highest potential by boldly walking the path together.

The Phoenix Rising:
How I Transformed My Greatest Pain into My Life's Purpose

By Baz Porter

"We gain strength, courage, and confidence by each experience in which we stop to look fear in the face...we must do that which we think we cannot." Eleanor Roosevelt

The Pivotal Moment

The image staring back jolted me - a vacant, hollow stranger somehow now my reflection. I knew this rock bottom moment marked a monumental turning point.

After years of inner turmoil - wrestling childhood demons, numbing with addiction, relationships crumbling - I had finally reached my breaking point. With nowhere left to run, I faced an excruciating choice: either cling to the dysfunctional coping mechanisms slowly destroying me or finding the courage to change course radically.

Summoning strength I didn't know I had; I chose growth. I could never have predicted how profoundly that courage would alter my life's trajectory.

My Metamorphosis from Darkness into Light

Like many, trauma's ghosts haunted my early years. The painful memories lurked within, waiting to ambush me when I least expected. No matter how far I fled outwardly, the anguish always found me in the end. I desperately sought relief in any form I could find - alcohol, drugs, adrenaline rushes. But the emptiness persisted no matter how much I numbed or distracted. I grappled to find any glimmer of meaning or purpose amidst the swirling darkness.

From the outside, I created a convincing facade of normalcy. I advanced rapidly in my corporate career, earning raises and accolades for top performance. I moved into a luxury high-rise apartment and drove a flashy new sports car. But inside, I remained broken, empty, and lost. No mask could cover the hollowness I felt.

Until that fateful morning - the vacant hazel eyes staring back jolted me to my core. A wave of clarity washed over me: I had finally hit rock bottom. With nothing left to lose, I bought a one-way ticket to America with my remaining $360 savings. Leaving behind everything and everyone from my past existence overseas, I set out on a solo cross-country tour. I had no plan, no direction—only a flickering desire to reinvent myself far from the ghosts that haunted me. I hoped the further I traveled physically, the further I could outrun my inner demons.

In each new city, I made connections by offering free life coaching and compassion to those battling hardship and trauma, from the homeless to the addicted. At first, it provided a welcome distraction from my pain. But over time, something shifted. Bearing witness to their struggles stirred an empathy I had long suppressed. Their willingness to open up lit a spark of meaning that had eluded me for so long. For the first time, I glimpsed a redemptive purpose, rising from the ashes of my agony. "Your pain is the breaking of the shell that encloses your understanding. It is the bitter potion by which the physician within you heals your sick self." - Khalil Gibran.

Discovering My Coaching Purpose

The breakthrough came organically one gray morning in a San Francisco alley. I was facilitating an impromptu session with a young man named Caleb, who sat slumped against a graffitied wall, eyes downcast and shoulders slumped in despair.

As I gently asked Caleb to share what brought him to such hopelessness, his story came pouring out in a flood. He spoke of childhood abuse, losing his parents, cycling in and out of jail, homelessness, and heroin addiction. Tears streamed down his gaunt cheeks as the pain poured from his shattered heart.

In that instant, the fog encircling me lifted. With sudden clarity, I realized overcoming adversity uniquely equipped me to guide others out of darkness. My sense of purpose crystallized like bursts of sunlight penetrating an overcast sky: to empower people to transform their lives despite hardship.

Walking with others as they courageously unearthed their inner shadows helped me finally confront my own. Holding sacred space for their healing journey accelerated my own. By bravely sharing my story, I built connections and community through shared struggles. It turned out my mess pointed me to my message all along. My passion for uplifting others emerged from the depths of my personal rock bottom. Before, I saw only brokenness and shame in my past; now, I have discovered meaning and medicine. The very wounds that once weighed me down transformed into wisdom to help lift others.

"Your purpose in life is to find your purpose and give your whole heart and soul to it." - Buddha.

My Coaching Philosophy and Approach

Through my metamorphosis, I saw boundless potential in every person, regardless of where or how they started in this life. Our past does not have to dictate our future. Our most significant wounds can become our greatest gifts with courage and willingness.

My methodology integrates personal development, mindfulness practices, and strategic planning to enable holistic growth. I guide people to live and lead purposefully from their heart's highest wisdom, using challenges as fuel to expand their potential.

My approach follows the R.A.M.S. framework cultivated through my own professional and personal journey:

Results

- Set bold visions as North Stars
- Maintain focused discipline
- Develop strategic plans
- Measure progress and celebrate wins

"Change takes place when the pain of remaining the same is greater than the pain of change." - Tony Robbins

Attitude

- Identify and transform limiting beliefs
- Cultivate resilience and growth mindset
- Turn challenges into opportunities
- Remain open and adaptive

Mastery

- Assess current capabilities
- Seek out mentors
- Commit to daily practice
- Become a lifelong learner

Systems

- Analyze and optimize processes
- Leverage technology
- Build high-performing teams
- Codify systems to scale

R.A.M.S. provides a holistic framework for sustainable success by developing inner emotional strengths and outer strategic execution skills. This allows me to support each client's unique leadership and life journey with customized guidance.

Together, we identify core values, set inspired visions, build critical skills, and execute excellently - while embracing an empowered mindset. By integrating all levels synergistically, breakthrough growth becomes possible.

The Ripple Effects of Service

Witnessing people reclaim their power and purpose remains the greatest joy of this work. By walking together through hardship, radical hope emerges.

In serving others, I found my healing. The trauma that once weighed me down now provides perspective to lift others genuinely. When you offer compassion without condition, you receive the gift of connection. I'm humbled and grateful for each soul willing to let me walk beside them through challenge and change. They gave me the gift of growth in holding space for their journeys. This work gifted me a new lease on life beyond what I imagined possible. When you give and serve freely, overflow returns.

A wise teacher once told me that darkness cannot drive out darkness; only light can do that. I now know my light was forged by walking through the darkness.

"Darkness cannot drive out darkness; only light can do that. Hate cannot drive out hate; only love can do that." - Martin Luther King, Jr.

Your Phoenix Story Awaits

If parts of my story resonate, I invite you to take the next step in your journey. Visit www.bazporter.com to schedule a consultation where we can explore your boldest vision while enjoying a warm cup of coffee. The time for change is now.

I look forward to learning about your dreams and how I may assist in making them a reality. Even the longest journeys begin with a single step.

The world needs your light.

Your most remarkable transformation arises from boldly walking through the fire and sharing your gifts fully. In overcoming, you will be empowered. From the ashes, you will rise.

Your phoenix story awaits, ready to inspire all those still searching for the courage to take flight. Our wings are formed by walking through the fire.

***

To contact Baz:

LinkedIn: https://www.linkedin.com/in/bazporterllc

Website: https://www.bazporter.com/leadership-coaching

www.ramsbybaz.com

Susy Francis Best

Empowering leaders to freely achieve their goals, dreams, and desires with joy while leaving a legacy of impact is what Susy Francis Best, PsyD MBA, lives for. Raised in the US Virgin Islands, Dr. Susy's early exposure to faith and resilience fueled her determination to understand the essence of true success and how to support others in achieving it.

Dr. Susy's work as a coach, consultant, and speaker has touched over 30,000 leaders globally, ranging from entrepreneurs to Fortune 100 professionals. Her proprietary THRIVE formula, grounded in strength-based awareness, continuous improvement, and mindfulness, has yielded measurable excellence in leadership, resilience, and well-being, guiding leaders to experience the transformation that leads to thriving at the highest levels.

For decades, Dr. Susy has blended her bilingual global corporate leader, strategist, and psychologist roles to create transformational experiences that allow individuals and teams to experience increased sustainable engagement, income, and impact. Balancing professional excellence with a genuine love for life, Dr. Susy enjoys time invested in her faith, family, nature, and homeland with a focus on civic engagement and philanthropy.

Whether you are an aspiring leader or an established executive, Dr. Susy offers a wealth of knowledge and strategies to unlock your true potential, exceed expectations, and make a lasting impact on your personal and professional journey of pursuing the "richness" of living life to the fullest.

Cracking the Rich Code: 7 Habits for Holistic Wealth

By Susy Francis Best

In the relentless pursuit of success, the quest for wealth often overshadows the richness of life in its entirety. This chapter explores five critical dimensions of holistic wealth and extends an exclusive invitation to explore the seven transformative habits that unlock holistic wealth. Comprehensive wealth goes beyond mere financial aspects to encompass every facet of our existence, including our physical, mental, and spiritual well-being, as well as our social connections and the use of financial resources to leave a lasting impact. We embark on a neuroscientific and faith-infused journey to crack the rich code.

Defining True Richness and the Call to Purposeful Living

"What does it profit a person to gain the world, yet forfeit their soul?" - Mark 8:36

What does it truly mean to be rich, and why do we relentlessly chase it? The pursuit of wealth often commences with a soul-stirring question about its essence. Imagine amassing a fortune only to be confronted with a terminal diagnosis. In those poignant moments, we stand face-to-face with the core of richness, extending far beyond material gains. It implores us to ponder what genuinely matters, including the dimensions of being rich in body, mind, spirit, influence, legacy, social relationships, and the tapestry of financial wealth.

Pursuing wealth is not just about financial gain but a call to purposeful living. Life's fleeting nature invites us to choose between the hollow regret of unfulfilled dreams and the fulfillment of intentional existence. Wealth then becomes a vehicle for a life rich in joy, peace, and purposeful legacy.

With decades of guiding clients, I've witnessed the transformative power of aligning one's purpose with one's actions. Whether we are talking about young professionals embarking on their journey or executives seeking fulfillment in later stages, the joy and peace in living a life of purpose are profound and unparalleled.

The Wisdom in Dying: Lessons from the Departed

Bronnie Ware's "The Top Five Regrets of the Dying" unveils profound insights echoed by those at life's end. Across cultures and ages, Bronnie's insights and research studies reveal that the departing wish for the following:

- The courage to live authentically
- Slowing down and choosing to savor life's pleasures
- Having the courage to be one's true self
- Investing time and love in meaningful relationships
- Choosing happiness over dissatisfaction.

These insights serve as beacons of hope, reminding us that it's never too late to live richly and forge a meaningful legacy. Often, we delay pursuing what matters, waiting for perfect timing or circumstances. Yet, the truth is, the perfect moment is now. It's better to start small and build momentum than to wait for perfection and accomplish nothing. The most crucial step is to BEGIN.

A defining moment in my career was working with a terminally ill, retired neurosurgeon. Initially skeptical of me, he was impressed by my honesty and chose to confide in me. His goal was to reconcile with his adult children and express the love he had never verbalized despite leaving them a significant inheritance.

Our sessions were challenging yet fulfilling. Eventually, he shed his self-imposed 'curmudgeon' label, embracing his true identity as a skilled doctor and a loving father. Our final meetings focused on the peace and joy he found in pursuing what truly mattered, accepting what he couldn't change.

I am blessed to work with many leaders seeking a holistic approach to life's zenith. Being part of the profound positive impact on individuals, teams, families, and communities is incredibly rewarding. Clients envision their best life, taking steps and cultivating habits to live their richest life and leave their desired legacy. They embody joy and peace that inspire others, a testament to the power of starting and persisting on this transformative journey.

The Holistic Richness: 5 Key Dimensions Body, Mind, Spirit, Social Relationships, and Financial Wealth

As a society, we have recently faced numerous global challenges in health, economy, and peace. These challenges have forced us to reconsider our way of life and our definition of wealth.

Currently, there is a flood of discussions and educational initiatives urging us to let go of the expectation of stability and embrace the new normal of life as VUCA (volatile, complex, uncertain, and ambiguous). The new VUCA norm calls upon us to develop resilience and embrace a holistic approach to richness. To embark on this transformative journey and incorporate the seven habits, we must first thoroughly evaluate our current state in each of the five dimensions.

It is important to be honest with ourselves and ask what we need to stop, start, and continue regarding our beliefs and actions. This self-reflection will help us achieve and maintain peak performance when incorporating the seven habits. To assist you on this journey, a free workbook is available. Information on how to access this workbook can be found at the end of this chapter.

1. Body: The Temple of Our Being

Physical fitness is foundational to our journey. Research shows a strong connection between physical fitness and overall wealth. Applying discipline to our vision, we nurture the instrument needed for the transformative journey—our body. Optimizing our practices of nutrition, physical exercise, hygiene, regular medical checkups, and minimizing or eliminating foods, drinks, and substances that cause harm will afford us the highest chance to have the instrument of our body in a peak performance state.

How ready is my body to take on new habits?

2. Mind: The Crucible of Strength

Neuroscience highlights the importance of mental and emotional well-being for personal growth. Focusing on mental health improves overall health and a more fulfilling, purposeful life. Regular meditation, prayer, gratitude, and a positive outlook have all been linked to improved psychological health, increased well-being, reduced symptoms, and enhanced behavioral regulation. Cultivating a positive mindset and emotional well-being can lead to a more fulfilling and purposeful life.

How mentally and emotionally prepared am I for the stop, start, continue journey I am about to embark upon?

3. Spirit/Influence/Legacy: The Spiritual Essence

Psychologically, recognizing life's spiritual dimension and connecting with a higher purpose provides an increased value of life. Pursuing mere pleasure leads to dissatisfaction and higher rates of life discontent and suicide. Historical literature and religions emphasize living to create a lasting, positive impact beyond ourselves, ensuring a fulfilling life legacy.

Globally, people report that prayer, meditation, gratitude, interacting with nature and music, and leveraging our time, talent, and treasure provide feelings of peace and joy, foster life satisfaction and influence, and leave a legacy.

How aligned are my values, desires, goals, and daily actions to my life's purpose?

4. Social Relationships: The Network of Support

Nurturing healthy family bonds and friendships is vital for holistic richness and satisfaction. Neuroscience attests to the importance of social connections marked by vulnerability, authenticity, and accountability and their ability to enhance well-being and success significantly.

Despite increased connectivity options, loneliness prevails, underscoring the need for intentional relationship-building. Relationships and collaboration are crucial in holistic richness, appreciating that self-love and acceptance mirror our capacity to form meaningful bonds.

Research shows that leaders who invest in nurturing self-acceptance and these social connections experience compounded benefits in their endeavors and overall well-being.

Do I have the sense of self-worth and the supportive network I need for this transformative journey?

5. Financial Wealth: A Tool for Legacy

Proverbs 22:7, "The borrower is slave to the lender," demonstrates that financial independence begins with living within our means. True wealth involves accumulating resources and managing them with intent and purpose, allowing us the freedom to care for ourselves and others as desired, thereby creating a lasting and meaningful legacy.

Is my income sufficient not only to cover my expenses but also to allow for self-care and contributions towards the legacy I aim to build and the causes I am passionate about?

Reflect on the five dimensions of holistic wealth and identify one impactful action that will propel you forward in embracing the seven habits of cracking the rich code. Remember, perfection isn't the goal – taking that first step is. Don't hesitate; begin your journey now.

The 7 Habits Unveiled: Cracking the Rich Code

Habit #1: Vision - The Power of Clarity

"Where there is no vision, the people perish." Proverbs 29:18

Vision is a critical catalyst in the journey to wealth. Far more than just a dream, it's the cornerstone of wealth creation, instilling confidence and precision in actions, and a viable plan for prosperity. Research supports this, showing a 70-85% higher success rate for those who actively document and revisit their goals.

Underpinned by neuroscience, the power of visualization with clarity, akin to physical practice, is a proven method of goal achievement. Understanding our current position is as vital as knowing our destination. Like navigating with Google Maps, the success of our journey depends on the accuracy of our starting point. Only with a clear understanding of our present can we map out a path to our desired future.

The journey to wealth starts with limitless dreaming. Envision the possibilities without constraints of time and money and capture your grandest dreams in a tangible form – through journals, drawings, vision boards, or the SMART (specific, measurable, achievable, relevant, and time-bound) goal format.

This unrestricted creative process opens doors to your deepest desires. The nature of your goals, whether financial, relational, or personal, requires consistent visualization. Picture your success vividly: its appearance, feeling, and transformative effect.

Begin your wealth creation with a crystal-clear vision. It's not just a guide but an inspiration for a future filled with endless possibilities. Remember, a powerful vision is the first step toward a life of abundant wealth.

"Leadership is the capacity to translate a vision into a reality." Warren Bennis

ACTION: Vividly imagine what achieving your goal will encompass – the look, the feel, and the essence of the accomplishment. Engage all your senses to intensify the experience of achieving your goal. Begin the process of creating the vision on paper in whatever format you choose.

Habit #2: Why - The Deepest Motivations

"Search me, O God, and know my heart: try me, and know my thoughts." - Psalm 139:23

Understanding the 'why' behind our goals is crucial for achieving true success. Often, people lose their way because they aren't clear about their motivations. When challenges arise, a strong, deeply rooted 'why' keeps us steadfast.

The '5 Whys' technique is a journey to the heart of our aspirations. It's not just about setting goals; it's about unveiling the profound reasons that fuel these goals, enabling us to maximize our potential, fulfill our purpose, and leave a meaningful legacy.

Start by stating your goal and ask 'why' five times. Each 'why' delves deeper, moving past superficial reasons to the core of your true motivations. This exploration often reveals deep emotions and clarity about the real wealth that lies in achieving your goals. For example, a client transitioning from corporate leadership to entrepreneurship discovered his 'whys' ranged from personal freedom to living out his true purpose and creating opportunities for others.

Reaching your core 'why' requires a positive mindset. Our thoughts shape our lives; nurturing positivity and excellence in our minds enhances cognitive function, creativity, and problem-solving. Leaders with a wealthy mindset choose thoughts that align with their highest aspirations, paving the way for success in every aspect of life.

"People don't buy what you do, they buy why you do it....Why did you get out of bed this morning and why should anyone care." Simon Sinek

ACTION: Identify a goal for increasing your holistic wealth. Courageously explore it through the '5 Whys,' giving yourself the time and space to uncover the deepest reasons driving your ambition.

Habit #3: Self-Awareness - Embracing Strengths and Weaknesses

"I praise you because I am fearfully and wonderfully made." - Psalm 139:14

Self-awareness is fundamental in wealth creation and sustainability, shaping our outcomes through understanding our beliefs and behaviors. This essential habit boosts confidence, creativity, and decision-making, which is essential for goal achievement and wealth building. Recognizing our strengths, weaknesses, and opportunity areas aligns us with our potential and fosters empathy and authentic connections.

In my leadership coaching, self-awareness assessments often yield transformative insights, aligning self-perception with external views and maximizing personal strengths. This heightened awareness is crucial for leveraging our abilities effectively, identifying potential obstacles, and clarifying goals. Clients employing self-awareness tools consistently enhance their success, embracing their true selves. The process incorporates a visual platform, deepening understanding of personal impacts and fostering growth. Embracing self-awareness is a powerful step towards holistic wealth, enabling a journey marked by authenticity and purposeful progress.

"Until you make the unconscious conscious, it will direct your life and you will call it fate." Carl Jung

ACTION: Reflect on your strengths and weaknesses or opportunity areas. Accept your true self and align your strengths with your goals. Seek honest feedback. Consider therapy or coaching with strength-based assessments for a deeper understanding, which can be instrumental in achieving your goals.

Habit #4: Discipline - Staying True to You

"Whoever loves discipline, loves knowledge." - Proverbs 12:1

Discipline is essential in aligning with our vision and purpose, forming the backbone of wealth creation. It's more than just aspiration; discipline is a commitment to our goals, safeguarding our path to financial freedom, health, or business success.

The challenge of discipline lies in overcoming the lure of instant gratification, a common trap in our culture promoting immediate fulfillment. This mindset often leads to financial pitfalls, including debt and its severe consequences. Discipline, therefore, is not just a practice but a mindset that guides us away from short-term temptations toward long-term success and fulfillment.

Incorporating discipline into our lives fosters financial prosperity and a mindset that benefits all aspects of our journey. It acts as a compass, directing us away from fleeting desires and towards enduring achievements and satisfaction.

"We don't have to be smarter than the rest, we have to be more disciplined." Warren Buffett

ACTION: Cultivate discipline by maintaining a clear vision and prioritizing long-term gains over immediate satisfaction. Create accountability, be consistent in your habits, and practice patience through delayed gratification. The results may not be immediate, but with perseverance, the desired outcome is within reach.

Habit #5: Strategic Planning - The Blueprint for Success

"The plans of the diligent lead to profit as surely as haste leads to poverty." - Proverbs 21:5

Strategic planning transforms aspirations into reality, requiring meticulous consideration of needs, timeframes, resources, and personnel. This aligns with the principle that diligent planning fosters prosperity.

Like a map, it guides us from where we are to our goals, anticipating challenges along the way. My experience shows that a robust strategic plan enhances efficiency and income in both corporations and personal ventures. Yet, many overlook its value, fearing its complexity, often leading to unmet goals. True success lies in embracing a realistic, comprehensive strategy that acknowledges our current state, sets clear outcomes, and leverages our strengths and weaknesses.

"People make their own luck (and fortune) by great preparation and good strategy." Jack Canfield

ACTION: Accept that success is rooted in disciplined, detailed planning. Create a comprehensive strategy, dividing goals into smaller steps and identifying easy wins and challenges. Engage a trusted advisor for insights and regularly review and adapt your plan. Embrace strategic planning as a mindset essential for achieving holistic wealth and your greatest ambitions.

Habit #6: Change Management - Embracing Growth

"Suppose you want to build a tower. Won't you first sit down and estimate the cost to see if you have enough money to complete it?" - Luke 14:28-30

The journey to your desired wealth demands persistence, adaptability, and the bravery to grow through change. Change management is about evaluating habits and staying clear-headed during transitions, embodying agility and a growth mindset. Both individuals and organizations often falter in executing plans, but effective change management can transform this, requiring an honest acknowledgment that goals necessitate change and adaptation.

Often, unmet goals stem from a lack of self-awareness and an understanding of the impacts of change. In our ever-changing world, the flexibility to pivot and regularly reassess our plans' alignment with our goals is essential for achieving success.

"Challenges are gifts that force us to search for a new center of gravity. Don't fight them. Just find a new way to stand." Oprah Winfrey

ACTION: Embrace the reality that achieving goals may require adjusting your approach. A growth mindset is vital, characterized by quick adaptation to change and unwavering commitment. Start with a clear vision, assess risks, and be prepared to realign your strategies. Never let circumstances derail you; stay focused, flexible, and agile.

Habit #7: Sustainability – Going the Distance

"Diligent hands bring wealth…money grows little by little." - Proverbs 10:4; 13:11

Sustainability in holistic wealth begins with foundational trust in a higher power and faith as the bedrock of success. Neuroscience shows that faith reduces stress, fosters resilience, and sharpens decision-making. Leaders grounded in faith confidently navigate towards true richness, guided by something greater than themselves.

Sustainable wealth creation is about embracing change, recognizing what no longer serves us, and aligning with our evolved identities. It's a journey of letting go of the past and embracing the new. True wealth extends beyond material possessions; it's about the lasting impact and meaningful legacy we leave.

"Be the change you wish to see in the world." Mahatma Gandhi

ACTION: Regularly assess and realign your goals and actions with your core values and beliefs. Actively embrace both the positive and negative aspects of change. Focus on creating a legacy that resonates with your true purpose.

Take Action: Crack the Rich Code

Accept that you can make your dreams and desires a reality and crack the rich code! Take a moment to contemplate the various aspects of holistic richness and envision your life with it. What will it cost you to stay the same? Identify one key action that will launch you forward. Perfection isn't required – just the courage to take that first transformative step. Start now and unlock the richness of life.

Ready to take on the 7 Habits for Holistic Wealth and make your desires a reality? Look no further than Dr. Susy, the ultimate coach for highly motivated individuals. With her guidance, she shatters limitations, exceeds expectations, and makes a lasting impact. Choose Dr. Susy for a journey of growth, action, and tangible results. Success is more than goals; it's a fulfilling life. Thrive in all aspects with Dr. Susy, leaving behind a remarkable legacy that inspires others to achieve the impossible.

Visit www.thrivegroupinternational.com to access the following free resources and to explore coaching programs, resources, and tools tailored to your unique journey.

- Take a deeper dive into the 5 Dimensions and 7 Habits for Holistic Wealth and Cracking the Rich Code: Download the FREE- Workbook (Type **7HABITS** in Promo Code Section)
- Get clarity on how to maximize the 7 Habits for Holistic Wealth: Access FREE- 30 minute clarity coaching session

Connect with Dr. Susy to join a community dedicated to unlocking full potential and cracking the rich code.

***

To contact Susy!

LinkedIn:	https://www.linkedin.com/in/drsusyfrancis
Facebook:	www.facebook.com/TheThriveGroup
Instagram:	www.instagram.com/drsusybest
Website:	www.Thrivegroupinternational.com
Email:	grow@thrivegroupinternational.com

Kim Malloy, Ph.D.

Dr. Kim Malloy is a business consultant specializing in organizational development (OD). She has a passion for helping leaders, managers and individuals thrive in both work and in life. Kim has a Ph.D. in Industrial-Organizational Psychology, and more than 25 years of experience in management consulting and executive coaching.

Her primary expertise lies in the areas of leadership development, 360 assessment, coaching, performance management, six sigma methodologies, and emotional intelligence. She has provided consulting and training services for companies across the globe, both individually and in partnership with such firms as TalentSmart, BTS, JONES Inclusive, and International Survey Research (ISR).

In her coaching work, Kim works with leaders to provide tailored feedback and developmental coaching through virtual assessment centers and 360 surveys. She has worked with hundreds of leaders within the U.S., as well as in Asia, Europe, South America, Australia, the Middle East and Africa.

For the past 18 years Kim has served as a volunteer for a non-profit, Operation One, where she has worked onsite and remotely with school leaders in Uganda, and with sponsored children who have been orphaned due to AIDS and other disease.

She received her master's degree and Ph.D. in Industrial-Organizational Psychology from the California School of Professional Psychology, where she also served as a visiting professor and adjunct faculty. She holds a bachelor's degree in psychology from San Diego State University.

Tackling Self-Doubt from the Inside Out

By Kim Malloy

"If you want to improve your self-worth, stop giving other people the calculator."

– Tim Fargo (Author, Entrepreneur)

Whether you're looking to enrich your life or to get rich in life, YOU are your greatest asset. But you might also be your own worst enemy. What you think about yourself matters and will directly impact how others perceive you. It's essential to know your value. And if you don't believe it, you'd better get to work because our thoughts and beliefs shape who we are. Period.

I've been working as an executive coach for almost 20 years, but it was only over the last ten years or so that it became the most prominent (and favorite) part of what I do. I've worked with many talented leaders representing different industries, job levels, and continents. One of the things that I love most about being a coach is that others will often share their innermost thoughts, challenges, and, yes, even their insecurities. The part that continues to amaze me, though, is that even the most successful (and seemingly confident) leaders will often express some degree of self-doubt, and it's often more extreme than you would expect.

These leaders come across as poised and confident on the outside, but there is often a layer of surprising self-doubt underneath. This is particularly true of female leaders, who seem more inclined to share their challenges with self-confidence and, at times, will label it imposter syndrome. This is not just based on my personal experience. There is a great deal of research on the subject. Some estimate that more than

70% of high achievers experience some form of imposter syndrome; the hallmark is that they generally keep it a secret.

After coaching hundreds of managers, leaders, and individual contributors, my work has led me to read about emotional intelligence, imposter syndrome, self-limiting beliefs, and more. I've realized that the more I learn, the more I still don't know. This is because humans are complex and beautiful. But I do know that regardless of the cause(s) of one's self-doubt, the key is to figure out whether it's getting in the way of success. If it is getting in the way, it's essential to understand "why" and identify personalized strategies and a meaningful path forward.

Your thoughts may be more negative than you realize

"What we can or cannot do, what we consider possible or impossible, is rarely a function of our true capability. It is more likely a function of our beliefs about who we are." – Tony Robbins

Whether talking about self-doubt, limiting beliefs, or full-blown imposter syndrome, all roads lead back to the voice in our head that is constantly asking, "Am I enough?"

While it's difficult to quantify thoughts, research has suggested that the average person has 12,000 to 60,000 thoughts daily. It has also been estimated that as many as 70% of our thoughts are negative, and up to 95% may be repetitive. In other words, we keep replaying the negative messages repeatedly. You can think of this as mental chatter. These negative thoughts will ultimately lead to limiting beliefs ("I'm not good enough," "others can do it better," etc.).

Neuroscientists suggest that negative thinking is hardwired into our brains. It's actually part of our survival instincts (our "fight or flight" response). It's sometimes also referred to as the negativity bias. Early in human history, paying attention to dangerous situations and negative threats was a matter of life and death. Those attuned to danger and threats around them were more likely to survive, and this genetic survival instinct has been passed down over time.

According to neuropsychologist Dr. Rick Hanson, "The mind is like Velcro for negative experiences and Teflon for positive ones." The key, then, is to figure out ways to get more positive ones to stick!

Imposter syndrome, also known as imposter phenomenon, is a psychological occurrence that is characterized by feelings of self-doubt, inadequacy, and incompetence. It is further exemplified by doubting one's skills and accomplishments, often to the extent that a person experiences a persistent fear of being exposed as a fraud. This psychological pattern affects many people, regardless of gender, race, or age. However, it is most often associated with women, who are more likely to experience it due to societal and cultural pressures.

As noted earlier, research suggests that more than 70% of professionals report feeling self-doubt or like an imposter at some point. And while it can affect anyone, it's more often associated with high-achieving women who are in male-dominated industries, as well as underrepresented groups in general. Recent studies have shown that men do also experience imposter syndrome but also indicate that they may be less inclined to talk about it or to seek help.

I'm not sharing all of this research to further foster the negative but to let you know that if you experience this type of thinking, you are not alone. Fixing it can feel like an uphill battle, but it is absolutely doable.

One of the most prevalent ways I see the "focus on the negative" is when having feedback meetings with my clients. A significant portion of the work that I do involves feedback, which generally stems from either a 360 survey or participation in a virtual business simulation. When it comes time to review the results, one of the things that happens (like clockwork) is that the individual immediately jumps to the negative comments and feedback. It doesn't matter whether the report is 80% glowing; they will automatically focus on the negative and downplay or dismiss all of the good stuff.

This could, of course, be viewed as a positive thing (from a continuous improvement perspective). Still, my concern is that they may be missing the rare opportunity to be validated and to understand and leverage their most important assets - their strengths. I'm a stickler on this one and will spend time reviewing and sharing my observations of their strengths. And I have to say that it's quite powerful to watch someone's body language and attitude shift as a result. They often report that they don't get enough feedback, especially positive, and that hearing it from someone who works with different leaders gives them a sense that they are doing okay.

While the subject is complex, a key takeaway is this: Negative thinking and self-doubt can and will get in the way of success. Don't let the "I'm not good enough" or "others deserve it more" hold you back.

Isn't a little bit of self-doubt a good thing?

> *"The greater the artist, the greater the doubt. Perfect confidence is granted to the less talented as a consolation prize." – Robert Hughes (Art Critic)*

So what!? Why does it matter if I experience self-doubt - as long as I show up and do a good job, nobody will know. As a matter of fact, one of my early learnings as a new consultant was to "fake it 'til you make it." And I did. I figured it out, and it was all okay. The key, I've learned, is to know when self-doubt is getting in your way versus motivating you to achieve.

A little bit of stress can be a good thing. Self-doubt can motivate us to keep learning and growing, and it certainly keeps us grounded and humble. It can also help to raise any red flags that we may not be doing our best work or that the work that we're doing isn't necessarily what we are best suited to be doing. I know that for me my insecurities constantly push and motivate me to do better. Complacency can be dangerous, and a little bit of self-doubt can push us out of our comfort zone, as long as it doesn't paralyze us.

There are numerous examples of famous people who have openly shared their struggles with self-doubt.

- Lady Gaga has openly revealed that she "sometimes feels like a loser kid in high school." She says: "It's crazy, 'cos it's like we're at the Garden, but I still feel like a loser kid in high school. I just have to pick myself up and tell myself I'm a superstar every morning just so I can get through this day. I feel like I have to fight. I'm fighting for every kid that's like me, that's felt like I've felt and feels like I still feel."
- Serena Williams, arguably the greatest female tennis player of all time, has openly shared that she struggles with self-doubt. Her advice to women experiencing self-doubt is to push past the limits they put on themselves. "Don't be afraid of the word no. It doesn't mean it's a bad result. It just means try again. You can't be afraid to ask, because if you don't, no one else is. If you just go out there and not be afraid of the negative result, you'll be surprised. You may get a positive result."
- Arianna Huffington has referred to the negative self-talk in her head as the obnoxious roommate. She says, "Educating our obnoxious roommate requires redefining success and what it means to live a life that matters, which will be different for each of us, according to our own values and goals (and not those imposed upon us by society)."

- There are many more examples of highly successful people who have overcome their own self-limiting beliefs, and you may have a few examples yourself. So, let's talk about how to quiet down that obnoxious roommate once and for all.

Overcoming self-doubt and limiting beliefs through Emotional Intelligence

"I don't want to be at the mercy of my emotions. I want to use them, to enjoy them, and to dominate them." – Oscar Wilde

The vast writings and research in emotional intelligence (EI) provide powerful insights and strategies for understanding and managing one's self-confidence and limiting beliefs. While 'emotional intelligence' has existed since the 1960s, it gained popularity when Daniel Goleman published the bestselling book Emotional Intelligence in 1995. Emotional intelligence is the ability to recognize, interpret, and regulate your emotions and those of other people. One of the most powerful aspects of the research on EI is that it is deeply rooted in neuroscience.

As a consultant, I've worked with various firms, including a company called TalentSmart. They specialize in emotional intelligence and are considered the world's largest provider of EI assessments and training. During my tenure there, I coached executives and facilitated training programs in emotional intelligence for companies and leaders worldwide. It was certainly an experience I will never forget. The power of EI is real!

Emotional intelligence as a skillset is typically broken down into four core competencies:

- Self-awareness
- Self-management
- Social awareness
- Relationship management

The first two competencies are referred to as our personal competence, while the latter are social competence. When addressing limiting beliefs and self-doubt, we will focus on personal competence (self-awareness, self-management). After all, we can only control ourselves! This means our thinking, behaviors, and reactions to our external environment and others.

Increase your Self-Awareness: Take time to reflect and understand.

"But feelings can't be ignored, no matter how unjust or ungrateful they seem." – Anne Frank

Self-awareness is your ability to accurately perceive your emotions and stay aware of them as they happen.

I often tell my clients that the keywords here are "accurately" and "as they happen." This is because our brain's reasoning ability can get slightly fuzzy when our emotions take over (i.e., an emotional hijacking). The adrenaline clouds our thinking, and often, what we think we are feeling isn't necessarily an accurate assessment of the situation.

Have you ever heard the term "hindsight is 20/20?" I know I've reflected on situations I thought I had handled perfectly fine, only to realize later that I was acting from a place of emotion, not reason. This is also known as emotional hijacking, which Goleman refers to as a situation in which the amygdala (the part of the brain that serves as our emotional processor) hijacks or bypasses our normal reasoning process. In other words, we let the emotions take over.

Another critical component of self-awareness is understanding how you typically respond to different emotions, people, and situations. For example, when you're overly tired, are you more sensitive to feedback from others? Do you do your best work in the mornings or at night? The more we understand ourselves and how we respond to the environment around us, the better we can navigate things to do our best work. This is about knowing our emotional triggers. In other words, what emotions or situations lead to an emotional hijacking?

The key is to know your emotional triggers. What are those things that immediately elicit a response, good or bad, and how do you typically respond to them? Triggers are typically based on a lifetime of experiences and differ for everyone.

For example, if you grew up with a critical parent, you are likely to replay that voice in your head by establishing a critical internal dialogue ("That was stupid," or "Why can't you be more like so and so?"). Over time, this dialogue creates stories in our minds that we typically don't even question. We just accept it as reality.

The best way to gain control over that voice is to pay attention to your self-talk (often negative chatter in your head) and be willing to question it. While those stories may have served you well in the past, they may no longer be an effective part of who you are today. So, pay attention to your internal dialogue, and when it does not align with or motivate you to achieve your goals, you need to find a way to stop it and reframe it into a positive.

Socrates believed the first step to true wisdom is to "know thyself," because only then can one appreciate what one understands and what remains to be learned.

Refine your Self-Management: Challenge yourself to think differently daily.

"If you hear a voice within you say you cannot paint, then by all means paint and that voice will be silenced." – Vincent van Gogh

Self-management is your ability to use awareness of your emotions to stay flexible and to manage your behaviors, thoughts, and emotions consciously and productively.

Self-management is ultimately about the effectiveness of our behaviors. It's not about right or wrong; it's not about holding in or stifling our emotions. It's about speaking up when we need to speak up. It's about biting your tongue when speaking up, which will not help the situation.

It's about CHOOSING how we respond to different situations and others.

If we believe that emotional triggers are hardwired into our brains, then we may need to do a bit of rewiring from time to time to ensure that we are responding with intention and purpose and in ways that are moving us closer to our goals.

I love the analogy of a large, grassy field. Now, picture a well-worn path through the field, which has been traveled time and time again. You can think of this path as the neural connections in our brain. Our responses to certain triggers become automatic because they have been hardwired into our brains.

To develop new automatic ways of responding to old habits, we need to carve out a new path. We must practice these new, productive responses over and over again to develop new automatic ways of responding to old stimuli and triggers. Research suggests that we need to practice something upwards of 100 times in order to create new habits or automatic ways of responding.

One of the premier thought leaders on emotional intelligence, Travis Bradberry, recently published a new book, Emotional Intelligence Habits. In discussing the book, he says:

"Habits are the compound interest of self-improvement. When you work on micro-behaviors, small things that are easy to implement every single day, you see big changes over time."

A Few Tips to Overcome Your Limiting Beliefs

There are numerous books and articles on the subject, but the most important thing is to figure out which strategies work best for you. Keep in mind that, to make lasting change, you need to make it a priority to both understand your patterns of self-talk and make it a habitual focus to change it.

I often refer to this as "mindfulness and intentionality." You need to be clearly aware and present in the moment to understand when and where your limiting beliefs are popping up (mindfulness), and then be intentional about changing the thought patterns that lead to self-doubt or limiting beliefs.

Here are a few quick strategies to get you started:

Know your Patterns (Self-Awareness)

- **Start by acknowledging the limiting belief; Pay attention to your self-talk.**
    - Don't ignore or push it away - just be aware of the thoughts holding you back.
    - Try journaling or simply tracking your self-talk and thought patterns for a few days. Is it generally positive, or is it generally negative?
- **Try to understand where it comes from**
    - Is there something from your past that has created these self-limiting beliefs (i.e., stories) in your head?
    - Is there something or someone in your life that continues to perpetuate these beliefs (i.e., triggers)?
- **Challenge it**
    - Ask yourself why you believe these thoughts; what evidence do you have to support them (or not)?
    - Are they actually true, or are they things you've assumed to be true without checking for accuracy?

Retrain your Brain (Self-Management)

- **Catch yourself in the act (mindfulness)**
    - Try to stay present in the moment that negative self-talk is happening.
    - Don't get hooked on the emotions that follow – it's okay to acknowledge them, but try to have the awareness to "talk yourself down."

- **Reframe your thinking (intentionality)**
  - This can help you to change your mindset (and reaction) in the moment.
  - Try to reframe any negative statements into positives.
  - Instead of thinking "I can't do this," try to tell yourself the reasons why you can,

- **Create a "mantra" or positive affirmation**
  - This might be a statement you repeat to yourself daily or a mantra you use when you're feeling triggered or experiencing self-doubt.
  - I've heard many great mantras over the years. These are typically quite personal, but some examples include "Stop it," "I got this!" or "Let go, let God."
- **If at first you don't succeed, try, try again**
  - This means that you won't get it perfectly right every time.
  - The key to increasing our emotional intelligence is to practice, practice, practice, and it will get easier over time.

While this article focuses on addressing self-doubt from the inside out, some strategies start from the outside in. In other words, surround yourself with champions. This can mean either spending time with those who believe in you or those who are achieving the great things that you aspire to achieve.

A final quote from Tony Robbins:

"To learn how to overcome self-doubt and climb to the peak of achievement, you'll need *people to lift you up. Find someone who has what you want and emulate them. Practice peer elevation as well: Minimize relationships that bring*

negativity into your life and surround yourself with positivity and support instead."

***

To contact Kim:

Email: kim@malloyconsulting.com
LinkedIn: https://www.linkedin.com/in/kimmalloy/

Victor Bullara

Victor ("Vic) has 40+ years of experience in the Coaching, Human Resources, and Leadership Development fields. Vic's experience includes 19 years as an HR practice leader for Ernst & Young, Korn Ferry, and DDI World where he implemented HR "best practices" at 21 Fortune 500 companies. He has coached, developed, and mentored 1,150 executives. In the 14 years before starting his executive coaching and leadership assessment/development firm, Vic held executive level HR roles at four, high growth tech firms with one growing from 7 employees to 400.

Education and Certifications

Victor has a degree in Psychology and Organizational Behavior from UCLA and taught HR courses at UCLA and UC Irvine for six years. He is a certified Executive/Master Coach, an International Coach Federation (ICF) Credentialed Coach, and a *Certified Winslow Dynamics Consultant.* He also completed (with "Distinction") the *Inspiring Leadership through Emotional Intelligence* program through Case Western Reserve University. He is a certified instructor and Master Trainer through DDI World. He is an Executive Coach to MBA students at UCLA's Anderson School of Management. He is also on the Board of Directors of Reality Smash, a virtual reality/AI content developer.

.

I Will Know It When I See It

By Victor Bullara

Ever wonder what an executive coach does? I am a certified master coach (which means I've been coaching for a long time and have racked up more than 3,000 coaching hours). I have coached senior leaders, board members, and "high potentials" since 2012. I thought this would be an interesting case study to address all the issues associated with a complex coaching assignment. Note that this case study and the model/practices listed to help improve this client's executive presence can be used in your life to do the same.

If I were to come up with a title for this assignment, it would be ***"I'll know it when I see it."***

> *This phrase is often attributed to Supreme Court Justice Potter Stewart. He used this expression in 1964 while trying to define obscenity in a case before the United States Supreme Court. The case was Jacobellis v. Ohio, and it dealt with whether the film "The Lovers" was obscene. In his concurring opinion, Justice Stewart stated: "I shall not today attempt further to define the kinds of material I understand to be embraced within that shorthand description ["hard-core pornography"]; and perhaps I could never succeed in intelligibly doing so. But **I will know it when I see it**."*

For several years, I have worked with a global accounting and assurance firm with more than 39,000 employees, of which 2,300, or about 6%, are partners. I have been working with their senior leaders and managing directors as their executive coach, where I would help them to identify and overcome obstacles to success, help them develop their leadership skills and abilities, and prepare them for a potential promotion to partner. One client, "Gabriella" (not her real name), had been with the firm for 13 years, often working 50 to 70 hours per week as all her peers have. Four years ago, she began conversing with her bosses about the partner assessment and selection process. Those conversations led to her enrollment in a series of firm training programs covering everything from technical competency to relationship building. A couple of years ago, she started having more formal conversations about building her book of business (revenue generation) and improving how she managed her client/project teams.

She was selected to participate in the partner selection process this year since she had met the essential criteria, including achievement of revenue generation goals and solid performance reviews year after year. Her clients loved her work, giving her very positive client satisfaction reports and feedback from her colleagues, and the client/project teams she had led were equally positive. She finally met with the partner selection committee for a panel interview where she would be grilled for several hours.

She thought she had done well but realized that not everyone was promoted to partner (typically, the odds are about 1 in 8 or 12.5%). She had received the news that she had not made partner, but her development plan to prepare for next year's process included getting help from an executive coach (me) to help her prepare for the next promotional cycle. When I first met Gabriella, she was not only disappointed, stressed, and also quite confused. The committee told her she lacked "executive presence." When I asked her what they meant by "executive presence," she said they never explained what that meant (hence the "I'll know it when I see it" reference). No wonder she was confused. As her coach, I found this to be a real problem in that I couldn't help her develop something that hadn't already been defined in detail.

So, what does the research say about *executive presence?* According to the Center for Talent Innovation, the founding president and CEO of the Center for Talent Innovation, Sylvia Ann Hewlett, described her groundbreaking research, the basis for which included hundreds of survey responses from industry leaders and "a ton of focus groups and interviews in terms of what is important to your boss" concerning EP came up with the following components of *executive presence* (EP).

A. 67% of EP consists of **how you act** (high performers who can't conjure up this secret sauce don't make it), described as *grace under fire, decisiveness, integrity, speaking truth to power, emotional intelligence, reputations & standing, pedigree, vision & charisma.*

B. 28% of the equation is **how you speak** (described as *superior communication skills, ability to command the room, forcefulness, assertiveness, ability to read the room, sense of humor & ability to banter, body language & posture.*

C. 5% is represented by **how you look** (described as *grooming & polish, physical attractiveness & being slim, sophisticated clothing & flair "dressing for your next job," height - "being tall" and youthful/vigorous appearance.*

Sylvia Ann Hewlett, a **Cambridge-educated** economist, said that "leadership roles are often given to those who look and act the part." Top jobs often elude women and professionals of color because they lack "executive presence," or underestimate its importance.

So, how did we help Gabriella's boss and her employer's partner selection committee grasp this concept of EP? We first met with the committee and conducted our research by asking for specific examples of EP in the firm.

What did these leaders do, say, and look like to demonstrate *executive presence? W*e were looking for examples exclusive of gender and race. We interviewed numerous partners, summarized our findings, and then confirmed them through focus group discussions consisting of Partners, Senior Managers, and Directors. Our conclusions came up with the following competencies (followed by key success behaviors):

Section 1: Complete Competency List

You can imagine how comprehensive the competency list became when speaking to such a broad audience. We came up with the following 11 competencies and then proceeded, with the agreement by the nominating committee and key partners, to limit the number and combine specific competencies.

1. **Confidence**: Partners need to project self-assurance and belief in their decisions. This confidence should be visible in their body language, tone of voice, and how they carry themselves.

2. **Communication skills**: Clear and effective communication is paramount. This includes not only speaking skills but also active listening, empathy, and the ability to tailor messages to different audiences.

3. **Poise and Composure: m**anaging composure under pressure is essential. Partners must remain calm, collected, and professional even in challenging or high-stakes situations. Authenticity: being genuine and authentic is critical for building trust with colleagues, superiors, clients, and subordinates. Authenticity fosters a sense of credibility and relatability.

4. **Charisma**: While it can't be forced, having a magnetic presence can help draw people in and make them want to follow your lead. Charismatic individuals tend to inspire and motivate others.

5. **Professionalism**: Partners must consistently exhibit a high level of professionalism. This includes appropriate attire, punctuality, and adherence to ethical standards.

6. **Emotional Intelligence** Understanding and managing one's own emotions, as well as being attuned to the emotions of others, is crucial for effective leadership. This involves empathy, self-awareness, and navigating complex interpersonal dynamics.

7. **Strategic thinking**: Partners must have a broad view of their organization and industry. They should be able to think strategically, set long-term goals, and align their actions with the overall vision of the organization.

8. **Adaptability**: In a rapidly changing business environment, adapting to new situations, technologies, and strategies is crucial. Being open to change and demonstrating a growth mindset is an essential aspect of executive presence.

9. **Resilience**: The ability to bounce back from setbacks or failures is an important quality for partners. Demonstrating resilience helps inspire confidence in their leadership.

10. **Global and cultural awareness**: In an increasingly globalized world, understanding and appreciating different cultures, perspectives, practices, and norms is vital for effective leadership.

11. **Conflict Resolution**: Partners often must manage conflicts within their teams or with external stakeholders. Having the ability to navigate and constructively resolve conflicts is a critical skill.

Section II: Abbreviated, Working Competency List

The list below became our working model for building a multi-rater assessment system.

1. ***Communication Skills:*** *Good Vocabulary and tone, concise, commanding, appropriate use of humor, professional frequency (pitch), good listener, good use of pauses, not verbose, quickly reads the audience and adjusts style as needed, persuasive.*

2. ***Posture/Body Language:*** *Professional appearance (consistent with work environments), appropriate eye contact, good use of gestures (consistent with intentions), calm, not nervous, image of confidence. "expansive" demeanor vs. (closed/crossed arms).*

3. ***Persona/Gravitas:*** *Personable, confident yet humble, credible, engaging, convincing, in control of emotions, present (in the moment), focused, poised, and calm even when "under fire," self-aware, driven by purpose.*

4. ***Establishes High Level of Trust (Clients/Partners/Team):*** *Builds and maintains trust, admits mistakes, is transparent at all times, is direct - does not speak of others behind their backs, delivers on promises, is highly trusted by all, and is authentic.*

Section III: How did We Assess Her Current Level of Executive Presence

1. **Behavioral Interviews:** We asked Gabriella to provide specific examples of situations where they demonstrated executive presence. Focus on scenarios relevant to the partner role she is being considered for, including influencing stakeholders or handling high-pressure situations.

2. **Case Studies or Simulations:** We created realistic scenarios or case studies that mimic the challenges she would face in the role. We observed how she approached and navigated these situations, including her decision-making process, communication style, and ability to maintain composure.

3. **Presentation Skills:** We observed Gabriella delivering presentations on various relevant topics. We noticed her ability to communicate effectively, engage the audience, and convey confidence in their subject matter.

4. **Panel Interviews:** We asked Gabriella to participate in mock interviews. This provided different perspectives on her presence, allowing us to gauge how she interacted with various levels of the organization.

5. **360 Assessment Tools:** We constructed a survey to gain insights into her interpersonal skills, emotional intelligence, and leadership style. We sent the questionnaires to partners, peers, team members, colleagues, and a few selective clients.

6. *Key Satisfaction Areas: In addition to the five steps summarized above, we asked Gabriella to assess her current level of satisfaction in the 12 specific areas. Some of these overlap with assessment areas in the other five steps, while some of them don't. Significant dissatisfaction can be a roadblock holding her back from becoming a partner. These areas included Financial Success, Leadership Ability, Working Relationships, Family Relationships, Level of Engagement at Work, Feeling of Personal Freedom, Communication Skills, Productivity, Time Management, Work/Life Balance, Health & Wellness, and Energy Level.*

Section IV: From Gap Analysis to Coaching Roadmap

We gathered all the data from these assessments and created a "gap analysis" (a process used to assess the difference or "gap" between a current state and partnership requirements. It is a systematic approach to identifying areas where there is a disparity between where Gabriella's skills (satisfaction) currently are and where she needs to be in order to be promoted to partner.

The six steps outlined were designed to provide Gabriella with specific goals (not just vague statements) for improving her executive presence. We took the "gaps" and created a coaching roadmap - how we will get from one point to another, with the destination being Gabriella promoted to partner. We had already agreed that this would be a nine-month engagement with two 90-minute sessions every month. We also agreed that we would meet face-to-face in my office.

Section V: Feedback Review

Summarizing the feedback from the sources in Section III, we found the following average scores (based on a ten-point scale with ten being the highest and one being the lowest):

Competency
   Gabriella's Average Score

Competency	Score
Communication Skills	5
Posture/Body Language	5
Persona/Gravitas	7
Establishes High Level of Trust	8

We divided the four core competencies (***Communication Skills, Posture/Body Language, Persona/Gravitas, and Establishing a High Level of Trust (Clients/Partners/Team)*** into discrete goals to be worked on quarterly (assuming a nine-month program, two sessions each month less start-up month and closure review month which equals a total of 16 working sessions).

"Start-up Session:

Before we reviewed the data, we talked about how she felt during the panel interviews. She indicated that she was extremely anxious before the interview, and during it, she felt extremely nervous. She thought she did not do her best, and these feelings were not typical of how she felt during even the most complex presentations, client challenges, or team meetings. Such feelings are quite common in the C-suite, according to research from Beeja Meditation, indicating that 22% of senior management staff and business leaders experience stress in the workplace every day, and 26% feel stressed several times a week. The conclusions went on to say that "an adrenaline culture to get stuff done that compromises physiological and neurological functions and underpins mental health issues, and there is a rampant culture of perfectionism that leads to negativity, misunderstandings, unattainable expectations, and a lot of negative self-talk."

We discussed this "negative self-talk" (or gremlins), and Gabriella indicated that she experienced these gremlins throughout her entire career. She also suggested that her position and employer emphasized perfectionism on every task, project, or client/employee survey. This *negative self-talk* is a major obstacle to high performance at all organizational levels, so we set out a plan to help Gabriella minimize the amount of *self-talk* that takes away from her performance. *Negative self-talk* statements include "I am not good enough," "I am lazy," "I am weak," "I am not smart or good-looking enough," "I am not capable," "It is not safe to let my guard down," "I have to change who I am so that people will like me," "I am not rich enough" or similar phrases. We agreed to the following plan:

Mindfulness practices

Tim Ferris, angel investor and one of Fast Company's "Most Innovative Business People," conducted a study of more than 200 executives, leaders, and world-class performers. He found that **more than 80 percent practiced some form of mindfulness or meditation.** Gabriela agreed she would start practicing self-compassion through mindfulness to rid herself of the *negative self-talk*. She would begin with journaling – jotting when she resorted to negative self-talk or experienced distressing situations. She agreed to write about how she felt as the negative thought or event occurred, recognize that it is part of common humanity, and end the entry by being kind to herself. People who practice self-compassion know and accept that they are imperfect but don't resort to self-blame or shame.

Steve Jobs was transparent about using mindfulness and meditation techniques to unleash creativity, gain clarity, and reduce stress during his time at Apple. Meditation allowed him to cut through the chaos of his environment and aggressively realize his vision. In his new book *Focus*, psychologist Dr. Daniel Goleman, the father of emotional intelligence (or EQ), provides data that supports the importance of mindfulness in focusing the mind's cognitive abilities, linking them to **qualities of the heart like compassion and courage**. Dr. Goleman prescribes a framework cultivating this type of focus by **establishing regular practices that allow your brain to fully relax and let go of the anxiousness, confusion, and pressures** that can fill the day. Mindfulness can help calm stress, depression, and anxiety, as well as increase productivity and creativity, and improve relationships and health.

Gabriella agreed to a daily mindfulness practice that would include daily pauses at random or fixed moments performing the three-minute breathing space. Take about 1 minute per phase: (1.) *Awareness*: She will ask herself, *"How am I doing right now?"* She will focus her attention on her inner perception. She will notice which thoughts, feelings, and physical sensations she is experiencing and translate them into words. For example: "There are self-critical thoughts" or "I notice I am tense." What are you feeling in your body? Allow yourself to feel what you are feeling in the current moment. Accept it - it is okay what she is feeling, and whatever is there is fine just the way it is. (2.) *Breathing*: Gabriella agreed to focus her full attention on her breath and follow the breathing with her attention. (3) *Expansion of attention*: She will allow her attention to expand to the rest of her body, following how her breath moves throughout her whole body. With every in-breath, she can feel how her body expands a little, and with each out-breath, how it shrinks a little.

Each Subsequent Session Begins with a check-in:

- How are mindfulness practices going? Any "ah ha moments?"
- Do you have any concerns about coaching that have come up since we last met? If so, what are they, and how shall we address them?
- Tell me about your successes since we last met.
- What have you found to be a challenge since our last session?
- Where are you on a scale of 0-10 in reference to this quarter's goal?
- What needs to change or happen to get to a 10?
- What are the possible obstacles that may hinder you from achieving the goal?
- How will you overcome the obstacles?

Section VI: Results

After nine months and a second round of assessments, Gabriella was able to

- *Increase her communication skills from a* **5** *to an* **8**
- *Increase her Posture/Body Language skills from a 5 to an 8*
- *Increase her Persona/Gravitas skills from a 7 to a 9*
- *Increase her skills in Establishing a High Level of Trust from an 8 to a 9*

Selected improvements in the 12 Satisfaction Areas listed in Section 3 included *Leadership Ability (from a 6 to a 9), Working Relationships (from a 6 to a 9), Level of Engagement at Work (from 6 to a 9, Communication Skills (from a 6 to a 9), productivity (from a 7 to 9) and Energy Level (from 5 to an 8).*

More importantly, she was promoted to partner at the next promotional cycle!

***

To contact Vic:

Vic@WorldClassHR.com

LinkedIn: www.linkedIn.com/in/VicBullara

949-235-2034

Schedule a complimentary, 45-minute strategy call at: https://doodle.com/bp/victorbullara/45-minute-strategy-call

Mary Hunter

With over three decades of experience, Mary Hunter has transformed businesses and impacted lives and people's hearts. Recognized as an acclaimed business and leadership expert, she holds multiple awards and was recently named an A-list professional to watch in 2023 by CRN.

Today, as the Founder of Empowering Your Future, she's a High-Performance Mindset and Business Leadership Coach. With 30 years in the technology industry and 20 years in leadership CEO roles, Mary excels at building and transforming teams that deliver and succeed in creating significant value for customers and shareholders in dynamic times. Having turned multiple loss-making business units into highly profitable growth divisions, she has an exceptional capability to care for and develop individuals simultaneously.

A transformational keynote speaker, she is passionate about inspiring audiences with actionable tools and techniques to enable them to drive change in their lives. Mary's engaging style, boundless energy, and extensive knowledge have made her a highly sought-after presenter.

Mary loves making a difference in people's lives. Supporting Tony Robbins as a trainer, she inspires individuals to unlock their full potential. She is committed to community impact and champions STEM (Science, Technology, Engineering & Maths) in schools and Women in Technology. She also sits on the Nottingham University Business School Advisory Board, embodying leadership that transcends boundaries for our future generation.

The FORECAST Model: Building Elite Teams That Win

By Mary Hunter

Having spent 30 years in the technology industry, including 20 years in CEO positions, I've led and grown many diverse and different-sized teams from across the globe. As I reflected on what works best to enable a team to be successful, I created the "FORECAST" model. Looking at the pyramid of core elements and building blocks from the base up, let's explore how it works:

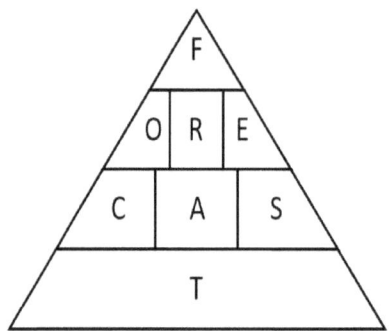

The FORECAST Model

T = Trust

Trust is the foundation and very heart of any successful team. Without it, there's less openness, sharing, and collaboration, which, in turn, means less innovation and less productivity.

Without trust, individuals spend time thinking of ways to protect themselves and their interests, so there is less time for confidence in taking action toward a common goal.

So, what does trust in a team really mean?

Trust is ultimately a safe place where team members can share their thoughts without fear of criticism, judgment, or reprisal, knowing that their opinions are valued and respected by others, and they can share and explore ideas safely to help the team achieve the goal.

Establishing trust can take some time. When a new team comes together, they need to get to know one another, and this initial investment in time is vital for long-term success. We come from various backgrounds and have different life experiences that shaped us into who we are today. Learning about one another and getting an understanding and appreciation for the team is a critical first step.

The great news is there are ways to build and accelerate the trust journey so individuals can become team players and the team can build momentum and succeed faster. The key to building relationships is to have multiple interactions and for colleagues to gain experiences together.

Team building activities and games can be used to build up trust. Opening up and sharing short stories about yourself is always a great start to bonding with a new team. I love to see new teams meet face to face early in a team's formation or when new members join, and through activities together, they can bond.

Many team-building games can be done in an office or an outdoor setting, enabling the team to gel with budgets that suit the company. Games are a great way to learn about a person and how they interact with others and uncover a person's real personality that may not be shared through a story.

From the initial meetings, the more time people spend together, the deeper connections will grow. Today, teams can come together virtually or in person, so regular team time invested is the key to accelerating relationships, building trust, and ultimately improving the team's performance. The greater the distance between the members, the harder it may be for a company to bring everyone together (from a cost and time perspective). However, I believe a minimum of two face-to-face meetings a year are necessary to ensure rapport and effective collaboration are maintained. These gatherings must allow time for team-building activities as well as working together so the team can flourish.

S = Superpower

We all have a superpower, our unique strength from our experience, that we bring to the team. Strong teams embrace one another's superpowers and see them as a competitive advantage that, together, is unstoppable. By leveraging everyone's strengths, confidence in all team players is unleashed, and from that, performance and productivity will thrive! As you shine the light on one another's strengths in a team, the heart of the team gains its beat, and momentum accelerates.

I love asking and learning about "who has what superpower?" If no one on the team has done "X," then we can expand the team by finding and learning from role models and looking wider for lessons learned that can help us grow and accelerate our journey - rarely are we conquering a task that has never been done before by someone, somewhere. Even if a skillset is in the group, it can be a great way to fine-tune and enhance your team's results using role models' lessons. So, the option to consider a role model and learn from them, even if you have some knowledge, is always there. You can turn decades of learning into days and support your team with a bit of creativity to be even more productive together.

If you have an egotistical person or a weak team player, they may feel threatened and view someone else's superpower as their personal weakness. Or they may want to focus on themselves and their strengths rather than appreciating the benefits or understanding their growth opportunity by surrounding themselves with people who can lift them up and help the team shine even more brightly. There is no letter "I" in TEAM, and that's because it's never about one person. It's about all of the group coming together to become a successful unit. A team is not where anyone should compare themselves to other members. It's about pulling together to achieve a common goal and supporting one another with the skills they have in the best way possible to achieve the shared purpose/mission.

A = **Authenticity**

People share when they believe there is rapport and a genuine interest from another person to connect. Being fully present in team meetings, having eye contact with your colleagues, being authentic to who you are, and being curious to ask questions to get to know them are ultimately the way forward. Connections form when we feel seen and heard.

Being authentically you and present in the moment is critical to any long-term relationship, whether that's business or personal life.

We can help accelerate connections through the questions we ask about our team members, how we think about them, and how we look at them. When joining a new team or when new team members have come into my team, a question I like to ask myself is, "what do I love about this person?" – none of us have walked a day in the life of someone else's shoes – we have no right to judge nor be judged by another person. By coming from a place of love, not judgment as I think about another person, I can always find something to appreciate and bond with, and that starts a connection that when I smile and think of them or indeed see them and look them in the eyes, they see my intent to connect. We can grow a bond, and trust will evolve over time.

Building genuine, authentic, trusting connections is vital to enable you to share, strategize, and gain maximum input, ideas, innovation, and ultimately success. The more you get genuinely curious about your team members, showing you care and want to get to know them or understand what they are saying, the more you will begin to form bonds, and this is when the team prospers.

From authenticity, confidence in your superpower grows, and from presence and building trust comes the ability to know you can ask for help and support as you won't be judged but are in a safe space where all are operating to achieve a common goal.

C = Clarity

Can you imagine a team where members need clarification on the outcome they are trying to achieve? How successful would you think they would be?

For any team to be successful, they need to be crystal clear about what they will achieve together. Clarity is power, and this means all the team needs to have the same vision, not a version or interpretation that is their meaning of the goal.

Ensuring everyone has the same meaning is the first step of the clarity journey to enable success.

A great way to do this, which can also support trust building, is to write the goal on a board and have the team share and discuss their interpretation of what this means. Once everyone is aligned on the goal, then clarity on the roles and responsibilities of team members should be explored next.

By asking questions in the team about experiences and passions and ultimately knowing "what superpowers they offer" and "how do you see these benefiting a specific role or activity that is needed to achieve the goal?" will enable the team to define roles and pull together to maximize the skills and knowledge they have in the group whilst placing the right team members into the right roles to deliver. While you're working through this clarity, understanding what motivates the team members to be here and why successfully achieving the goal is important to them can support the team's cohesion and placements.

E = Egos

Sometimes, in a team, we find an individual with a personal agenda. They are focused on themselves, what's in it for them, and how they can accelerate their career journey versus the wider team achieving the common goal. While they can sometimes smile and nod to the team, they may choose to operate in their silo and focus their input and attention on the leader of the team for their gain.

Any such behavior should be nipped in the bud as soon as they're observed. E.g., it may be perceived that someone rolled their eyes as another team member spoke and shared their thoughts, or they may interrupt and overpower the conversation and change the direction to suit themselves and their agenda. This can be upsetting and off-putting to the wider team as they see there is potential "judgment/lack of respect" happening within the group, and team members may question whether it is also safe to speak out. Any team member working in this way must be stopped fast, and the situation must be discussed for the team's long-term success. It could be a genuine mistake or misinterpretation, but if it's not questioned and clarified, then they risk by their behavior the silencing of other team members who fear they will be judged/cut off, and there's no point to their participation either, so the team starts to withdraw.

Whilst in a corporate team, it is rarely openly discussed, the reality from decades of research is that the majority have two primary fears:

1. I am not enough.
2. I won't be loved.

Some negative behaviors from people with strong egos can immediately bring these primary fears to the forefront of some team members' minds, and this often results in them retreating from activities and participation, negatively impacting the task at hand and, ultimately, the whole team's success.

It is imperative in a trusting team model that any action that does not support the team as a whole is always looked at, and thus, everyone can focus on the task at hand with 100% participation from the entire team. If you set your rules of engagement upfront, then it's likely that any team member will feel empowered to ask your team questions in a non-confrontational way to resolve any concern.

If no one else does, then this is where the team leader must step in and give feedback. The key is not to shy away and tolerate any ad hoc non-serving behaviors; otherwise, the trust in the team will be diminished, and cracks will form (see the Rules of Engagement and Feedback sections for how this can be dealt with).

By dealing with any situation fast, as soon as it happens, you can stop it whilst it's small and not let a problem grow and upset the workings of the team.

R = Rules of Engagement

Creating rules of engagement upfront is essential when a new team is formed. This brings clarity to the team members on expectations of behaviors that will and won't lead to success and ways of working that will or won't be accepted in the team. Pre-framing these in a "challenger" question that can be used to highlight any slip from this model of engagement enables a safe way for any team member to ask a question to challenge with team goal intent in mind an action/activity they don't believe is serving the whole group. It can be as simple as: "Will it enable our team to succeed?"

This is a simple, straightforward, direct, and non-confrontational question that any team member is empowered to ask whenever they feel a behavior or action is not serving the group to achieve their goal, and they'd like the team to pause and consider it further.

In the previous section, the example of dealing with an ego person in the team's behavior could be approached using your rules of engagement framework; the whole team knows the intent is coming from a great place to serve all, and someone's over-eagerness or maybe the "I" focus can be resolved instantly.

Celebration is also a key component of engagement. Having a team practice to celebrate one another's successes along the journey will build further momentum for the team, as well as the bonding of the group and their appreciation for one another.

Setbacks will occur in any team's journey. Being thoughtful and open on how these will be handled is imperative as this sets the tone of the culture everyone is operating in and, in reality, if they will feel able to take a risk. To have trust in place and a supportive solution-orientated approach where lessons are constructively learned versus a blame-focused culture is needed.

O = Open Listening

I've always loved having an "open microphone" when brainstorming – what this means is everyone says what they are thinking, no matter how small/incubating the idea or thought may appear to them. In this way, we trigger massive brainstorming from the wider group, and something small can evolve into another idea or accelerate into something amazing quite quickly.

Initially, when teams come together, there will always be some quieter people in the group who find it more challenging to share their voice and thus their ideas; using written communication to start e.g. a shared board or post-it notes for keywords and idea sharing initially will aid this and on occasion may also be used too. In this process everyone writes their ideas down first, and these are then reviewed and may be grouped together in themes with ideas and meaning discussed and shared. This is a fantastic way to get every member of the team's voice heard and all engaged and pulling together as a team. You may also want to consider anonymous idea sharing every so often too.

We know trust is not built overnight. However, you can accelerate a team's journey by supporting them to all take part in ways they are comfortable doing and by enabling them to do more activities together where they need to all work together as a team.

Being present and listening to one another's opinions is a key skill and part of any winning team formula. Listening may sound obvious, but many people listen to respond to someone versus listening to hear, consider, understand, pause, and then respond. By listening more sincerely, the team can all feel genuinely heard, and their opinion can be fully considered. This action will increase the likelihood of more of the team actively sharing their views and more valuable discussions for the greater good of innovation and collaboration. During brainstorming, you may consider a silence period of 10-30 seconds after each new idea is heard. This will enable the idea to be deeply considered and usually results in thorough consideration and exploration afterward.

F = Feedback

Be open to giving and receiving feedback from all members of the team. Feedback is a gift when shared from the heart, and the person's input is based on a positive intent to achieve success for a common goal. Many times, we actually don't always consider every person's role on a team at a given moment in time, and nor can we know what's going on in all areas, so sharing feedback and having an external perspective to one's own can actually benefit the team more than you might think. There are many different feedback models. A couple of key points are to show compassion whilst being honest and direct in your feedback. Don't dress it up so the person is not clear on the meaning you are trying to share but do consider how you would want to receive the feedback in a thoughtful, caring way. As a team, I think it's great to agree on regular feedback times and a model you all align with. Like the rules of engagement, this is about aligning intent. Whilst giving positive and negative feedback through alignment, you are giving opinions constructively. All members know the intent is honorable and the reason is to enhance individuals' performance to enable achievement of the goal together. Once feedback is received, the receiver may ask for clarity if they are not clear/do not understand the feedback. Still, you may set a rule that for developmental feedback you should not argue back to the person delivering the comments or feel the need to be defensive; they can simply say thank you and take the feedback under their consideration.

Let's talk straight. Feedback can be a great gift that may accelerate success and enhance performance and productivity; it can sometimes be unhelpful as you may think it's irrelevant or the person does not have the bigger picture and perspective. When you say thank you and take time to reflect on feedback, there can sometimes be a nugget of gold you might find that serves you and the team by taking action accordingly. Other times, you may decide the thank you is complete, and the feedback is not helpful nor relevant, given the facts you know to be true. The key is listening and considering based on the intent to add value to the team. Feedback will always come from a person's model of the world and what they know of any situation. Therefore, consideration is the key to what you do with it and what you embrace or discard. I personally find that if feedback has bothered me, there's usually a piece of truth in what's been shared that I can learn from.

A trusting connection with effective collaboration from all team members is ultimately the goal we are looking to make for any successful team. Trust becomes the beating heart and foundation upon which success can be built. From here, with all the other building blocks explored, i.e., the rules of engagement, roles, responsibilities, vision aligned, etc., effective creativity and collaboration with fun teamwork can thrive, resulting in an elite team that wins together.

***

To contact Mary:

This chapter is a summary of the FORECAST model and how to build elite teams that win. To learn more about the model or other business leadership services that Mary offers, go to www.empoweringyourfuture.co.uk

To book a discovery call and explore how to work together please connect with Mary via your preferred channel:

Message on LinkedIn: www.linkedin.com/in/maryhunter/

Or email: mary@empoweringyourfuture.co.uk

Adriana Gattermayr

Adriana Gattermayr is a Brazilian human development professional who began her career as a marketing consultant. Working with companies such as Avon, HSBC, Philips, IBM, and Nestlé for over ten years, she climbed up to VP of the marketing agency DMKT during its expansion to New York.

With an MBA from the renowned University of São Paulo, her career took a turn as she founded the non-profit Baraeté Institute. The organization focused on sustainability education and impacted hundreds of people through fun activities. Working with volunteers and their passion made Adriana grow her interest in understanding more about people and their motivations.

While studying at UC Berkeley, Wharton, IBMEC, and ICI, she developed research in corporate kindness that was later featured in several media vehicles and led to her collaboration as a video columnist for the business magazine Exame.com.

Adriana's success brought her to Head of Coaching for the SELAM region in the global consultancy BTS, where she reached a C-suite level with her coaching skills and became a member of the Forbes Coaches Council. Currently, she designs and delivers development journeys, coaching, communication workshops, and wellness journeys for Forbes 500 companies worldwide.

Mother of two lovely girls, Adriana is a writer of published books on non-fiction, fiction, and children's stories who loves to laugh, dance, and travel.

Strength and Honor: Whatever Happened to Empowering Teams?

By Adriana Gattermayr

Gladiator is one of my favorite movies of all time. If you have watched it, you might remember that the general played by Russell Crowe, the man himself, uses an empowering greeting with the members of his army: "Strength and honor." I have always loved this small and intense signature for the punch it has. It summons most of what we need to succeed in life. Nevertheless, it represents values on the verge of extinction, eaten up by society's need to crush every discomfort, lock up pain in crossfit gyms, and label every human being based on their behaviors and choices, only to establish an "us versus them" culture. This creates a world of infinite whining and victimism, the opposite of personal power and abundance.

Humans are simple creatures. We seek happiness and avoid pain, which our brains are wired to do. What we haven't figured out yet, at least most of us have not, is that although our 3D versions are simple, our soul is complex. Very complex. It doesn't fit inside labels, much less in small boxes of self-pity. Yet, this is how we are developing our companies' culture, this is how we are raising our children, this is what we are feeding our brains: smallness. How can we thrive in such a poisoned environment? We can't. We don't. We crumble, burn out, yell at those around us who are whining, and end up in a coaching session because our colleagues told our boss that we are "hard to deal with."

There seems to be a global misunderstanding of what harmony means, what respect involves, and what a healthy environment looks like. Strength is understood as a skill as opposed to harmony or just a synonym for resilience. It is not.

Honor is a skill not used anymore, substituted by consistency and honesty. It is more than that.

When workers try to establish a healthy environment in this context, they seek the absence of conflict and everlasting harmony. This is not a healthy environment, and no one is willing to talk about it because this truth might hurt some people's feelings.

Strength comes from your personal power and authenticity. When I talk about power, I don't mean negatively, like crushing others metaphorically or relying on the hierarchy/money to force one's way. Personal power is the internal fire lit up when you are confident of your skills and supported by your values and purpose. This is the true power, which works the same way in a collective, like a team, for example. Strength also encompasses resilience, a fashionable skill.

Why resilience by itself is not enough to empower oneself? Because resilience is passive. It is about endurance. We take whatever is thrown at us, stand up again, and keep fighting. Strength is active. It is about not letting daily problems bring you down. And what fuels all that is your power. Of course, all three are needed in the long run, yet we seem to forget this internal knowledge.

What about honor?

It feels tied to last century's gentleman duels. Nevertheless, it is what prevents us from creating a toxic environment. Much like strength, honor encompasses a myriad of concepts. It is about consistency, transparency, honesty, ethics, personal branding, and boundaries. In its true meaning, though, honor is this understanding that one is here to do the right thing.

Building up a successful team is much like building up an army, a metaphor that combines our thirst for the warrior archetype and the feeling of battling when working. However, what we see in the corporate world is much closer to the French court in Versailles than the Crusades. Interpersonal skills and learning to deal with big egos are just as crucial as delivering results. Here is where harmony and respect are much needed but cannot come at the cost of the team's strength and honor. They *depend* on strength and honor.

Harmony cannot be built without personal power. They will look a lot more like people-pleasing and empty corporate language if we move to force a healthy environment without this solid foundation. To make this even more complicated, I'll tell you now that my definition of personal power is incomplete.

All major corporate training, HR policies, and high-performance gurus speak of the leaders' duty to empower their teams. Their teachings cover all the basics: clear purpose, correct setting of goals, regular feedback, positive recognition, abundant communication, and so forth. They are all important, no doubt about it. So why do we all feel like we are stepping on people's wounds whenever we try to communicate with a group, even if we are following the basic empowerment steps? Why is everyone so angry all the time? Why is it that no matter how carefully we try to choose our words, someone is always offended, disempowered, annoyed, or hurt? Is it true that our society has become more sensitive by the hour? I don't think so.

There is a key called *choice* – and it seems to be missing.

A healthy environment at work, with harmony, respect, and inclusion, depends on an evolution of interpersonal relationships, which can only be achieved with internal work. That is correct. To live better with others, one must first live better with him/herself, which is the difficulty. It takes effort, it takes time, it takes will. When we talk about purpose, this is the real deal: our purpose is to evolve, not to find excuses for our own poor behavior. It is very easy for me to hang on the wall a purpose to make life better for all and complain about my colleague who was direct in giving feedback to me, saying they were rude. This is *not* living the purpose. This is not using strength. It is not living with honor.

You may wonder why I am talking about choice. It may not feel like it, but we are in charge of how we feel twenty-four hours a day. If someone is annoying, it is because we let them annoy us. If something is irritating, it is because we perceive it as irritating. If a team member pushes your buttons, you are allowing them to do so. I know most of us are aware of this truth, but understanding it in the mind is different from living it in the heart and in our actions or reactions. Here is where our power, strength, and honor make a difference. By using these skills, we can work on our shadows individually and as a team to learn to act and react in the most appropriate way – for you, others, and your goals. This means that emotional intelligence depends highly on developing our strength and honor.

Interestingly, when questioned about triggers and negative feelings, most of my coachees blame not the other who took away their peace but the fact that they are not Buddha. Precisely. I don't believe anyone alive is a Buddha, but that should not stop us from working on ourselves. Nevertheless, it is used as an excuse to make others cope with the coaches' lousy behavior. They don't know that this kind of thinking harms themselves a lot more. One of the executives I was working with last year used to repeat at least five times each session, "This is me," oblivious to the fact that we build the "me" we want to be. When confronted with that fact, he would decree, "They know how I am; they are used to it." Are they? Is it a good thing to have people not expecting more from you? How much do you lack the strength and honor to accept such low standards for yourself?

In my coaching practice, I see leaders doing their best to achieve results and make people happy. This is what business schools and HRs teach, right? And they do deliver results. More and more. Nevertheless, at the end of the day, nobody is happy. I don't mean happy in general, as most people like their jobs and their employers at a minimum, at least. I mean happy with what was achieved, even when they reach their goals. There is always a sense either of defeat for not reaching the end of the journey (since the core of each goal nowadays is to be a steppingstone for a bigger one and not quite a goal in itself) or a sense of urgency of "what is next?". Obviously, a company cannot park on a single goal and forget to grow. Still, there is an understanding amongst executives that growth is something totally detached from the reality around us, and this vision creates an imbalance, as the companies must feed the investor's never-ending expectancy.

Why is balance difficult? Because it is not something we achieve; it is something we cultivate. It is dynamic and reachable only in the present moment, the one that doesn't exist - or the *only one* that exists - the moment we are never in.

Here, we have the two pillars that sustain our most fulfilling work life: balance and choice – especially the choice we have about our attitude. Talking about challenges, they are the dragon-kings precisely because balance depends on making the right choices, which depend on our strength and honor. So, it all comes back to these skills that form our personal power. That is why empowering our teams is so important: it creates engagement and increases productivity. That is also why empowering our teams is so difficult.

Balance, for example, states that sometimes the company will not grow, just as we have days and nights, summer and winter, ups and downs. Choice means that when I get offended, it is because I choose to be offended by something or someone, for instance. You will argue that just because we have ups and downs does not mean the company shouldn't push for growth or our teams should not aim for more. Just because we choose how we feel does not mean the other person or situation is not offensive. Correct. Only that all this is irrelevant on a personal level.

For the individual, it doesn't matter if the other was offensive; it only matters if you will take the offense, give away your power, toss it out, and stand in your truth – *if you will exercise your strength*. It doesn't matter to the individual if the company's goal is detached from reality. What matters is your choice about the imbalance - *if you will stand in your honor*. If you join the imbalance, there is a price in mental health to pay.

This is all very beautiful, but how do we bring back strength and honor to a workforce that is so weakened? If you feel offended by the word *weakened*, you just proved my point. It is here to show the symptoms and help everyone to stand up on their feet and not depend on the goodwill of others. But before we jump into the how, be mindful that we are here speaking of a *complement* to the efforts of the collective to teach the workforce not to be clearly rude, offensive, mean, prejudicial, or any of this sort. To rely only on personal choice and let people say whatever they want to others is also not the answer – we had many decades of that to know it by now. Also, it is essential to be mindful that prejudice is not simply an offense; it is a prejudice in a worse level of despicable behavior and, therefore, requires a whole other level of internal power not to be absorbed. It is up to the non-victims to *understand* the reactions of those facing this struggle. Not to be condescending, not to tolerate retaliation or revenge, just understand and keep working collectively to extinguish all kinds of prejudice.

In working to empower teams, it is vital to create a safe environment first. Amy Edmondson, professor of Harvard Business School, teaches us that such an environment is built with a culture where workers can speak freely of concerns and fears, point out mistakes, and have support in fixing what is (or could be) wrong. There is no blaming game in such culture: the focus is on solving problems. By extracting the fear of the team's equation, leaders can bring back members' strength - as mistakes no longer mean weaknesses. They are simply part of the process. A culture like this is built with consistency and quality conversations with team members individually and as a group, which brings to the surface the "lack of time" problem.

I don't think I've ever had a coachee who did not complain of lack of time, and shortage of headcount is rarely a cause. It is first a status, then a lack of skills. Saying no is a skill. Setting boundaries is a skill – and please don't use hierarchy as an excuse. Taking control of your calendar is a skill. Developing new ways of working is a skill. Prioritizing is a skill. Based on this perception, a team with no psychological safety is one whose leader is not skillful. Plain and simple. That is why leaders must step into their power and honor their responsibility. By doing that, they will be able to control their time and develop the skills they need to do so.

Having quality conversations with team members is the single most crucial task the leader has to create power and protect the unit from toxicity. Once you have established such an environment, you must challenge your direct reports. Not make them happy, but challenge them with understanding, support, clarity, and honesty. Challenge is the exercise to create strength and honor muscles. There is a catch, though. Challenges must be in the exact measure that stretches reports to a point they can grow, not to the point that they break or give up before trying. Exercising strength will give a sense of "I can do more than I thought I was capable of." Exercising honor will give a sense of "My values, boundaries, and purpose are protected." This is what will bring satisfaction.

You did read the last paragraph right. It is not your job to make them happy. This is *their* job. Your job is to challenge them, support them, and coach them. It is also not your job to make them miserable or feel unsupported, so make sure you understand this difference.

Our M.O. as leaders in the current reality is to make life for us and our directs as easy as possible, joyful as possible, and peaceful as possible. It is a noble pursuit but a wrong one. I know you may find me bitter. Nevertheless, research shows that the more we search for happiness, the more miserable we feel - like the work published in Springer Link in 2018 (*Vanishing Time in the Pursuit of Happiness*, by Aekyoung Kim and Sam J. Maglio). This effect comes from trying to understand happiness as a destination and a conditional one: "I'll be happy when…" - it is, instead, a choice. A choice for the here and now, detached from the situation you are in and highly dependable on the mindset of finding beauty in the small things. This means not thinking about happiness but rather feeling joy in the present. How? By acting on what experience creates that for you and finding gratitude in what you have. This is what brings a sense of long-lasting happiness.

Paradoxically, knowing that you are not responsible for other people's happiness will free you time to work on scenarios that can bring them joy and support while helping them deliver results. It will also put you naturally in a coach/mentor mode that will aid them in becoming powerful authentically. And magically, this brings you power as well.

Remember that giving them support does not mean you are making things easy for them, nor that you are protecting them from offenses, insults, pressure, workload, and office politics. It means you are handing them challenges you know they can overcome, and that will require a lot of internal effort, which is different from stress. Stress and anxiety are issues one must overcome themselves and have little to do with what is happening outside. It has to do with what one is thinking of themselves. It's a lot like being offended. I can choose not to take something as an insult as much as I can choose not to stress myself out with an insane workload. Is it hard? Definitely. However, if we lose sight of it, we end up falling back into smallness.

Growing is painful, and working is hard. And yet, pain and challenge can feel good in a gym, right? So, let's train our brains to look at challenges as a means of strength and honor. A path to happiness. A good pain.

Our focus as a leader, therefore, is to:

1. Create psychological safety, banning fear and blaming from the process of innovation and problem-solving.
2. Challenge the team members to grow – and growing is not joyful as a process. It is uncomfortable. In the end, though, it will bring a sense of flow and satisfaction.
3. Push them to take accountability for their feelings, actions, and reactions.
4. Aim to give them support, direction, coaching, and feedback. Not happiness.

And the most important one: celebrate achievements together. Small, medium, big, great. Celebrate and remind people this is all for us.

***

To contact Adriana:

www.adrianagattermayr.com

contact@adrianagattermayr.com

www.linkedin.com/in/adrianagattermayr

Yarona Boster

Yarona Boster is an Advanced Certified Life Coach and International Speaker in the areas of Parenting, Loss, Infertility and Trauma. For over 17 years she has studied and worked in the fields of early childhood, psychology and coaching. Additionally, Yarona is an accomplished TEDx Speaker and Certified Speaker Coach who works with speakers the world over to hone and deliver their own TEDx talks, keynotes and more.

In addition to her parenting podcast series "The Evolution of Parenting," her parenting book, "Unspoken Signals," will revolutionize the way parents learn essential skills to raise emotionally secure children.

If you are looking for a coach who can provide emotional and intellectual support and incite real, sustainable change, Yarona is the coach you need. If you're searching for a speaker to engage and effect an audience on a multitude of levels, Yarona is most definitely the speaker to hire.

As the daughter of a Holocaust survivor, having suffered acute losses and multiple traumas herself, Yarona believes we are all trying to live a life of purpose in the finite time we have left.

The Investment Every Parent Needs to Make

by Yarona Boster

"*As a parent*, what is the one thing you want to KNOW, before you leave this world?"

Before I ever ask this question of my clients and audiences, many parents are under the assumption that their job is to set their children up for long term financial stability, success, and even generational wealth. At the very least, they believe it's their job to ensure their children's physical needs are provided for once they are gone.

In fact, this is usually the basis for most developed societal structures. If you have progeny, they are your physical responsibility until they come of age and are legally considered adults. That responsibility entails providing a roof over their head, clothes on their back, food in their bellies and a basic education.

Yet, once I ask the question above, they almost unanimously answer:

"I want to know that my children will be okay without me."

When we dig deeper together, we uncover that "okay" isn't about financial success, career accolades, having money in the bank, or even having a family of their own. It's the security of knowing that their child will have the emotional stability to live a healthy, whole-hearted life, after they're gone.

So, my follow up statement is: "then it all STARTS, with THAT end goal in mind." I love seeing the "aha" moment for them, the dynamic shift in their thinking, and a willingness to get started to ensure their children's emotional security is at the forefront of everything they do as parents.

Because true wealth is in the emotional investment we make in our children.

During our lives, the best thing we can hope for is that our children will outlive us. And one thing vital to our well-being as ordinary people trying to do our best as parents, is the security of "knowing." The result of truly healthy parenting is the knowledge that though they might miss you terribly, feel a wealth of pain, sadness - even moments of deep despair or depression - your children will eventually be able to pull themselves out of that pain and carry on without you.

Knowing our loved ones will be ok without us is THE goal at the end of our lives.

After years spent in the world of loss personally and professionally, there's a situation I've witnessed during the end stages of a person's life. If their life is not cut tragically short, there's usually a period when they're facing their mortality and their body is ready to move on, yet they still cling to life. There are countless stories of a person surrounded by loved ones, everyone wondering when that person will take their last breath. In those moments, someone will say it's ok to let go, or "I'll/we'll be ok," or something similar, and THAT will be the moment, or shortly after, they finally let go.

I experienced this with my father. He'd been in a state of unconsciousness for a week. As we cared for his body, carefully administering the hospice medications and sat by his bedside chatting nonsensically, we waited for the inevitable. The night before his passing, I sat quietly beside him taking "my turn" in the care shift and began to speak. I told him "Abba, I will be ok. I am happy with my life, so you don't need to worry about me. I'm happy with Carl and we'll live a happy life together."

Because my father had a dark sense of humor, I also asked him to please hold on until mid-day of the following day. Since we disliked the on-call nurse from hospice and more than that, we wanted to give him proper mourning time, which we wouldn't have been able to do by our customs if he passed that night. The following day, at noon on the dot, he took his last agonal breath. My father – a Holocaust survivor raised by German Jews - was nothing if not punctual.

For me this was a sign, as it is for so many others who've loved and lost. While we might not know what the future will bring for our children, or how the world will change once we're gone, if we have a sense of surety that our children will survive and truly be ok without us, it's peace of mind unlike any other in this world as we pass into the unknown.

Consequently, we cannot continue to talk about "IF" we die, we must talk about "WHEN."

Yet, as a professional in the fields and studies of early childhood development, psychology, and coaching – and as a parent, the child of deceased parents, and someone who's experienced excessive loss throughout her life - here's something I've noticed about the human condition.

Very few families are willing to have the deeply emotional conversations around death, terminal illnesses, and the dying process. These conversations often come during times of crisis, in hushed tones and hurried manners. During this time, when everyone is trying to figure out how to ensure their children will have reliable caregivers, financial stability, and a roof over their heads, the conversations of their emotional security are often set aside for their physical needs. Sadly, these emotionally fraught discussions are relegated to the bottom of the pile of importance when they need to be at the very top.

I once heard a story about a married couple. The wife had cancer and was actively dying. They had 3 young children: a nine-year-old, seven-year-old and five-year-old. The husband decided not to tell them their mother was dying, wanting to wait until after she passed. He wanted them to only have fun, happy memories of their mother. He also didn't want to burden his dying wife with the emotionally painful experience of seeing her children hurting as they processed losing her.

From all the evidence I've examined and immersed myself in over the last nearly two decades, it's my belief that in making that decision, he did his children the biggest disserve. He removed their ability to process losing their mother while she was still here to be a part of that experience. He took from them the possibility of finding some measure of comfort, alongside the painful reality of accepting she was leaving them and there was nothing they could do to change the outcome. If they'd had that, they might have been able to crystalize some of the memories with her in a way that "blissful ignorance" never truly can. Having her there while they worked through their feelings would have also helped cushion some of the blow of the loss they were about to experience.

You see, when we are aware of the finite nature of something, our appreciation of that thing becomes magnified. There's a reason we have sayings like "you never truly know what you have until it's gone." Impressively, children have a greater capacity to be "grateful in the moment" because of their "living in the now" mentality. This ability gives them a healthier process for dealing with their grief in a way that ensures healing and acceptance happens simultaneously with their heartache. Additionally, young children are especially "emotionally flexible." So, while you might fixate on your feelings, digging into them, unable to let them go, children are quite adaptable to accepting their feelings at face value and moving forward.

Here is an example of a child's capacity to accept loss and grieve simultaneously. We recently lost my father-in-law. My 5-year-old son was able to look at how it made him feel, express that with me, and find ways to reframe the loss with greater acceptance. I'll never forget the moment he said, "it's so sad and it hurts my heart. But maybe since Grandma and

Gapka fought sometimes, it's not TOO sad cause they'll no longer fight." Later, during the funeral services, he quietly whispered "I love you Gapka, I hope you loved me too." With tears on my face, I assured him that the love between them would never die, even though his grandfather was no longer here to express it.

These days, I'll ask how he's feeling about Gapka to see if any emotions are surfacing which he might need to process. It's best to have people there to support children while they journey with grief and loss, even while navigating our own. Giving children space to express their emotions and thoughts in a non-judgmental environment also gives them a deeper capacity to identify and express their emotions and use coping mechanisms to process them in a safe setting. Truthfully, this is a need for children and fully grown adults. We all need to express and explore our feelings surrounding loss, whether with one person or many, because real connection with others is a core component of healthy development.

Ultimately however, it's not our responsibility to "fix" our children's thoughts and feelings. Because while we might see them as a problem to be solved, it's the responsibility of the individual to determine how to resolve their feelings for their own well-being. Most importantly, it's our role as their parent or caregiver to provide them with the tools they need to do so.

Additionally, I belief managing loss is a life-long journey. Unlike the belief that the grieving process has a beginning and end, I've witnessed and experienced grief as a "rubber-band cycle." When it first happens, it's a tight, restrictive band around our heart, snapping painfully with every breath. However, over time, the "band-like effect" loses some of its "elasticity," or restrictiveness. And as the course of life unfolds, and we move further away from that loss, the rubber-band effect continues to loosen its agonizing grip on our hearts. Every now and again though, something snaps the band back into place, and the same feelings surface, replicating the initial moment we first experienced it. But with time, and each breath, that painful constriction begins to loosen once again.

Remarkably, when it comes to the inevitability of death, some parents have at most an idea of a plan in mind. They might discuss what should happen with their children's care if they die before their child becomes an adult. At the very least, they may talk to family or friends to ensure they've had a verbal discussion and promise that someone will take their children in, meeting their basic care needs. Some parents will even have something in writing attesting to this plan, and some will ensure there's a financial plan in place to safeguard their child's physical care needs.

Of course, this is completely dependent on the parents' financial and familial means. If parents don't have a support network, or the financial means to secure their children's care, that's a whole other loss for children to deal with: the loss of physical security and stability. This can be so overwhelming to even think about as a parent, some will avoid addressing these issues and metaphorically hold their breath until their children become adults.

When facing the inevitability of our demise it's easy to say, "I'll deal with this another day." But once you have children, creating a plan encompassing the physical, financial, and emotional needs of the children, ensures some of the loss they're experiencing isn't additionally burdened by decisions to be made in times of grief. This is the investment every parent needs to make to truly secure their children's future in the most ideal way possible.

Luckily, it's never too late to start on that plan. Here are some of the best steps you can take to ensure your children's emotional security is purposefully linked to their physical and financial security needs after you're gone.

Start in small measures with conversations about the finite nature of things. For example: their personal responsibilities and what we in the world of child development call "self-help skills." That means they need to learn how to do things for themselves. When they complain and ask why they must do it, please refrain from saying "because I said so." A simple explanation is that every person must know how to care for their own needs so they don't have to rely on another person and can do it on their own when no one else is around. Encouraging their confidence in their ability to do things for themselves is vital here too. Please refrain from criticizing them when they make mistakes, because with practice comes improvement and security in their competency to do it on their own.

Then you can explore the emotions this brings up for them about not always having you there. It's vital to explore those feelings without minimizing them. When they say, "mom, you'll always be here for me, right?" the simple response is "no, I won't always be here, but I'll always be in your heart." In fact, I do this with my son and have been since before he turned 4 years old. It doesn't "fix" his sadness, but it does help him more readily accept the finite nature of our time together.

Make no false promises to your children like "I'll always be here for you" or if they've asked you directly about death: "I won't die for a VERY long time." You can't control that, and it just makes the pain of sudden death or a speedy terminal illness worse, because you broke a vital promise. Young children take this very literally and it's the first step in recognizing your role in setting them up for emotional successes or failures.

Additionally, conversations about the finite and ever-changing nature of things will allow your children to accept it as a given when they're older. These conversations will get deeper and more complex over time, and you won't always have an answer. It's important to acknowledge that though you don't necessarily have the answers to all the questions they might have, you can talk about what you personally believe in, and they will find their own answers too. Once my son asked if I thought heaven was in the sky. I said I believe heaven is all around us, in nature, in our loved ones, and deep in my heart. He said, "I think heaven is in the sky," I said, "okay bud, that's cool" and the conversation moved on.

It's vital to have regular conversations with your adult children too. When my mother was dying, we had a conversation with the hospice workers I'll never forget. She believed I didn't know how bad things were with her cancer. She wasn't fully cognizant and had clearly forgotten I was her medical proxy and even had access to details she didn't, since I was coordinating her care. I believe she was trying to protect me from the reality of her situation. We had a long talk, cried, and hugged a lot that day.

While we'll never be fully prepared for the wealth of pain dealing with a loved one's death holds, there are ways to mitigate some of it, beginning with these kinds of conversations.

Now here are some of the technical action items you can do to ease the burden on your loved ones. The greatest gift you can give someone you love is to ease the burden of making the decisions around your demise.

Ensure someone you trust is given Durable Power of Attorney for you. This will allow them to make decisions in the event you have a life altering event that leaves you unable to make decisions for yourself medically or financially. Make sure you've discussed a range of possibilities, i.e. you have a stroke and need daily care, do you do that at home with your partner or at a long-term facility?

Have a fully discussed, written out plan for an "Advanced Directive" or "Living Will." Ideally a copy will be with your partner, adult children, the hospitals closest to you, and a lawyer if you have one.

Include details such as the time frame you'd want to be on life support with brain activity and life support without brain activity. I have "6 months to 1 year" in a coma or coma-induced state with brain activity. If there's no brain activity, I don't want to be on life support any longer than it takes to make the necessary arrangements.

Importantly, if you change your mind about what you want at any point, that information should be updated and discussed as well.

Have a Last Will and Testament written and as above, it should be discussed verbally with the documentation held in all appropriate locations. With underage children confirm you have any steps needed written out to ensure they're cared for and all measures are in place to meet their financial needs. Of primary importance, confirm the person/people who will become the care providers are willing and able to take those steps at any point. As with everything else, constant communication around these matters should be on-going, and the documentation updated accordingly since life can change from one minute to the next.

Lastly, discuss and prepare for funeral and burial arrangements. Check your state/country's allowances for pre-death preparations. Some will let you plan everything prior to your demise. This way the details aren't left to be hashed out by family members, and possibly fought over. These are YOUR wishes, end of story, no arguments or family rifts needed.

When we love people, relieving them of the burdens above allows them to focus on the loss and their grief without the added encumbrance of clashing family members who want different things for your dying/death plan. This will help your family, and ultimately your children, concentrate on what truly matters: finding comfort and healing in the aftermath of their loss. Ultimately, it is the best investment we could ever make in the well-being of our children and loved ones to ensure they can carry on without us.

***

To contact Yarona:

yarona@footprintscoaching.org

www.footprintscoaching.org

www.linkedin.com/in/yarona-boster-footprintscoaching

https://www.facebook.com/profile.php?id=100086807306793

https://www.instagram.com/yaronaboster1/

https://www.youtube.com/channel/UCh2JOJCN0zdamHAxGWaPbqA

Alba Contreras Rodriguez, MBA, PCC

Alba Contreras Rodriguez, MBA, PCC is owner and president of FONS (Focus on Solution), LLC where she provides executive, team, and group coaching to help leaders and organizations excel and implement major transitions and transformations. Influence Digest recognized Alba as one of the Top 15 Coaches in Detroit in 2021 and Corp! Magazine awarded her Most Valuable Entrepreneur in 2022.

She is a former global operations and management executive for Fortune 500 companies General Motors Corporation and Ford Motor Company, and a former management consultant for KPMG. Alba has a reputation as a visionary leader; a proven history of building high-performance teams; and expertise in establishing operational excellence within culturally and generationally diverse environments.

Alba is an International Coaching Federation Professional Certified Coach (PCC) and a Global Team Coaching Institute (GTCI) Certified Practitioner in Team Coaching. She received her MBA from the University of Michigan, Ross School of Business, where she co-founded the Ross Executive MBA Women's Initiative. She is also co-chair of Inforum's Mosaic Affinity Group; and served on the board of directors for the Cancer Support Community, and Madrinas; launched the Women's Network in Mexico; and led the Ford Women in Manufacturing, and the Ford Hispanic Network.

Fluent in Spanish and English, and conversational in Portuguese, Alba enjoys traveling, reading, music, dancing, and international cuisine, and loves being a wife, mom, and grandma.

Use Your Strengths to Enrich Your Life, Not Sabotage It

By Alba Contreras Rodriguez

Out of the blue, I was approached to co-author this book about cracking the rich code. My first reaction was, "I have no interest in writing about getting rich," which of course, is the default when we want to avoid something we are afraid of—we push back and find the reasons why it does not make sense to even consider it. As I started to expand my comfort net, I realized that we all want to crack the code to have a richer life, a more fulfilled life that makes us feel that "we have arrived." I was probably avoiding writing about it because of perfectionism.

My parents saw me as a child who needed to be overprotected because I was a girl and much younger than my two older siblings. I also had the natural ability to be very talkative and caring, with lots of pleasing and niceness so they thought I was the perfect child.

Then, the perfect child's parents went through a divorce, so I became a premature leader at a very young age—the one taking care of Mom and trying to still be nice to the father she loved but felt betrayed by. As I look back, there was a gap from childhood to adulthood—there was no time for being a typically headstrong adolescent. I felt I needed to be fully present, the best that I could be, and have the aspirations to go to college to become a great professional.

Right after I finished high school at sixteen, my mom made the courageous decision to move us from Venezuela to the United States so that my younger brother and I could learn the English language. Why, you ask? My grandpa on my father's side, a very intelligent and visionary man, had the conviction that if you spoke two languages, you were worth two people. My mom wanted to grant his wish that her four children would be bilingual.

In August 1978, we moved to Lawrence, Kansas to study English as a Second Language at the University of Kansas, leaving my older siblings behind because they were already bilingual. At that time, I only knew the English alphabet after a three-month crash course that my mom booked for all of us; her diplomacy and politeness did not allow her to push back on the teacher who would tell us, "You will know why it is so important to know it." When we landed in Miami as the first stop towards our new adventure, the immigration officer asked, how do you spell your name? At that moment a light bulb went on and I could connect the dots of what Ms. Atale had taught us.

The first thing I focused on once we got settled was taking the TOEFL test to be able to enroll as a freshman in the school of architecture. I thought I needed to get a 550 score and on the first attempt I got 500, so I continued studying until I got 570 and was admitted. The perfectionist in me thought the lower score was unacceptable when I could have started with it.

By January 1979, I started taking physics and calculus thinking that numbers would make it easier to understand English but was I wrong. I also couldn't see as progress the fact that I had made it to college in only four months, nor that I had facilitated getting us settled in a small town. I focused on my low grades in those quantitative subjects. Good enough was not good enough. One of the signs of exhibiting perfectionism is that we set such high expectations for ourselves and others that not only are we very harsh self-critics, but also, we are difficult to work with because it is hard to meet our standards, something my professors probably experienced with me.

As I changed majors, graduated, and worked in multiple industries and companies, I did not notice how much I was encouraged to aim at perfection so that I would be able to go up the corporate ladder and be recognized and rewarded for delivering high excellence. I was giving 120 percent consistently, at a speed and quality that no other person could. Remember, I was worth two people. I could do it, I had to do it, and failure was not an option if I wanted to stand out in very crowded, male-dominated environments.

My other instilled value was the importance of being caring and pleasing and always bringing others along for the ride without expecting anything in return. My mom taught me life was like a boomerang—anything I would throw, positive or negative, would eventually come back to me. My choice has always been to be positive, nurturing, and a good supporter and helper for others. As a corporate leader, I often wanted to make sure my team was cared for, which sometimes had negative effects for them and me because I did not delegate enough, thinking they'd be better off if I protected them from new and challenging responsibilities.

This nurturing trait was exhibited with my family as well. I overprotected my children to keep them safe when I could not be present because I was busy working to fulfill the dream to stay in the United States and give them a brighter future.

At the time, I did not know I had misused and overused two strengths: perfectionism and nurturing.

Defining an overused strength

We overuse a strength when we take it to an extreme. Then, it can become a weakness, even a liability. An overused strength is a derailer, a blind spot, a saboteur that typically shows up in moments of high stress when we feel hijacked, overtaken by negative emotions such as fear, anger, frustration, or shame.

What I did not realize early in my career is that people thought these strengths of getting things done with excellence, delivering results, and creating things nobody had before while being a nurturer at the same time were all goodness and benefit, but they were not when I overused or misused them. These traits weren't even labeled as strengths; they were considered natural abilities you were born with. Once those abilities started to be recognized and rewarded as strengths, there was a lot of incentive and upside to leveraging them. Something that was not good for me was encouraged and expected. And as a woman of color, I needed to be 'beyond perfect' and 'very nice.' Books like Lois P. Frankel's *Nice Girls Don't Get the Corner Office* continued sparking my curiosity as to why I felt stuck during my professional journey, but more about that later.

What escaped me was that going above and beyond meant I was overusing my strengths. Overused strengths are not obvious, and we are encouraged to overuse them. For me to realize that was a huge step because I had no idea what it was doing to me and others. I was so focused on corporate life—to achieve more and more to get to the dream—and that impacted my work-life integration. Instead of finding time for self-care, I would work for two people and be paid for one. I even decided that I needed to get an MBA while being a full-time executive to achieve more. My life was filled with work and responsibilities, but it wasn't a fulfilled life. That is why there are times I don't remember what my kids' homework struggles were as my wonderful husband was tracking that for us. I do know I tried to go to every sport or class event, sitting on the bleachers wearing my suit surrounded by stay-at-home moms who would brag about their homemade cookies versus the ones I had bought at Costco. Was the dream achieved? Absolutely, we became USA citizens in 2006. Was there a cost? I am sure there was, including multiple guilt trips on my side.

I invite you to pause and reflect. Identify a strength you have and think about how that strength serves you during moments of high stress. Reflect on how it shows up for you and for others. Think about two key words—intention and impact. You may have the intention of being very attentive to details but the impact on others is they may perceive you as a micromanager. You may have the intention of being highly independent but the impact on others is they see you as unable to build a team. You may have the intention of being confident, but when you show up as overconfident, the impact is you may be perceived as arrogant. You may have the intention of being ambitious to the point where others feel that you are overly ambitious and are pushing them.

During our personal and professional lives, we hold onto our strengths and proudly wear them as shining armor that makes us feel powerful and influential. We fail to recognize what Marshall Goldsmith's famous book says: *What Got You Here, Won't Get You There*. One key area I coach my clients on is transitions and helping them increase their self-awareness to see that what made them successful may not continue making them successful. For example, many leaders feel proud to have been rewarded and recognized for being great problem solvers. Once they get to the executive ranks of leadership, it is difficult for them to get out of the weeds and have the trust to delegate problem solving to their teams so that they can focus on the bigger picture. We focus on their mindset shift, rebranding, and moving from the playing field to the sidelines. This type of work is scary and difficult because it requires leaders to get out of their comfort zone so that growth can happen.

The cost of overusing your strengths

In 2011, Robert B. Kaiser and Darren V. Overfield conducted research to address the fact that managers turn their strengths into weaknesses through overuse. They coined the term "lopsided leadership" meaning "the pattern of a manager overdoing a strength at the expense of an opposing but complementary skill, competency, or perspective." They also started the dialogue that "there is such a thing as too much of a good thing."[1]

The consequence of excessive reliance on our strengths is a cascade of unintended outcomes and significant costs that vary from person to person.

Emotional consequences:

- Anxiety and worry
- Reduced self-esteem and confidence
- Difficulty in maintaining work-life balance

Physical consequences:

- Fatigue/Low energy
- Muscle tension and aches
- Digestive problems

Social consequences:

- Decreased social interactions and isolation
- Difficulty in forming new connections
- Reduced empathy and understanding toward others

Cognitive and behavioral consequences:

- Decreased problem-solving abilities
- Reduced ability to adapt to change
- Lack of mental clarity and focus

As an executive coach, I find that many of my clients, regardless of gender, show perfectionism tendencies but they may not exhibit those behaviors from their intent alone; they may be exhibiting the behaviors of the system they represent. I know how it feels to be in their shoes. The organizations I navigated in expected perfection and niceness, and I went with that flow by emulating what I thought would help me go up the corporate ladder. Also, there is a cultural system that influences what we do. As a Latina, there is more fear of failure masked by resiliency, and we are told to take care of others first and that everything we do is not about "I" but "We." There are many aspects of our lives that our culture and upbringing shape and influence, but that does not mean we cannot change and transform.

Feeling stuck

Rather than going up the ladder at the speed I thought I deserved given the results I was delivering—and being worth two people—I realized I was stuck. It was time to act and change internally to become unstuck. I had to focus on my own development and start doing the uncomfortable work I had been coaching and mentoring others to do. It was no longer about having the right sponsors and marketing myself; it was about identifying and breaking my limiting beliefs and becoming more self-aware of my strengths and how they were helping or hindering me.

I decided to hire an executive coach—the best investment I would ever make. She made an assessment and asked me to journal and to read *The Gifts of Imperfection* by Dr. Brené Brown. In my journal, I wrote, "Now I can see what my biggest opportunity is. It is called perfectionism." Brown said, "...we are too afraid to put anything out in the world that could be imperfect. It is also all of the dreams that we don't follow because of our deep fear of failing, making mistakes, and disappointing others."[2] And I thought, yes, that's exactly it!

Dr. Brené Brown has studied perfectionism for years and defines it in the book as "... a self-destructive and addictive belief system that fuels the primary thought that by being perfect we can avoid painful feelings of shame, judgment, and blame. There is no such thing as perfect. Perfection is an unattainable goal. Perfectionism is more about perception."[3]

While journaling, I envisioned my future: being a role model, leading a company, and making important contributions by helping others. I saw myself giving speeches on stage and my photo gracing magazine covers. I saw myself making a difference and leaving a legacy. This vision started to become a reality when I decided to become a coach to help other leaders see what I see in them and allow them to get out of their comfort zone to achieve their highest potential and aspirations. I wanted to replicate for them the transformational experience I had with my executive coach to help me get unstuck.

Roadmap to take action

You can try to avoid overusing your strengths, but that only treats the symptoms; you must go deeper. I give my clients this series of steps to prevent excessive utilization of strengths and to build new muscle memory.

Step 1: Increase self-awareness

It is essential to identify your strengths so that you can either leverage them or manage them. There are different ways to accomplish this including assessments, feedback, and performance evaluations. You can also use your own introspection by journaling. Identify one strength at a time and how it shows up during moments of high stress and think about how it serves you and others. Journaling is instrumental and has helped me and my clients access deeper thoughts and feelings.

Step 2: Set the dimmer switch

Think about a strength as a dimmer switch to know when to dim it up and when to dim it down. Learn to recognize when it is too much, the right amount, or too little relative to your job, organization, family, or community.

Step 3: Define a goal

Do not work on multiple overused strengths at once. Select one strength that you know you are overusing or misusing and define a clear goal for how you want to make the mindset shift to change the behavior. State the goal in a "from-to" format. For example, transition from being too attentive to detail to being a big picture thinker by delegating more to others.

Measure your stress level on a scale from one to ten (lower is better).

Step 4: Identify obstacles

Consider what obstacles could get in the way of achieving your goal and how you will avoid them or remove them when they show up. Choose who will support you and how you will stay committed to yourself and the goal.

Step 5: Act, measure, and reflect

Now that planning is completed, the natural next step is to act.

Review your stress level and see where you are at. Get feedback from others as to what they have noticed. Reflect and ask yourself what differences have taken place. Think about what you have learned about yourself and others during the journey and what may need adjustment. Decide how you will keep the momentum you've gained.

Step 6: Repeat

Go back to step three and define another goal for yourself. As you continue this process, it will become second nature, and you will not even think about the steps—you will have built that new muscle, and you will be using the dimmer switch to regulate the use of your strengths.

Closing thoughts

Everyone wants to crack the code to have a richer and more fulfilled life in which they experience a deep sense of satisfaction and purpose but overusing their strengths can sabotage that.

Many leaders know this, but it is hard to accept. They mainly think of leadership development as working on their weaknesses because their strengths are what they have been rewarded and recognized for, regardless of the consequences. Thinking about the dangers of overplaying their strengths can be unsettling because they fear losing their edge, their brand, their success. The opposite is more likely—excessive reliance on strengths can lead to career setbacks and failure. To stop overplaying your strengths does not mean to stop using or leveraging them; it means being more strategic and intentional in dialing the dimmer switch high or low.

Focus on your growth and transformation first, and everything else will get transformed. The ripple effect of your actions will be enormous and very rewarding. You will feel lighter and happier, and you will experience a richer, more fulfilled life.

Reach out if you need a thought and accountability partner and a sounding board. That is how I serve as a coach. I know how lonely it is the higher you get up that ladder.

***

To contact Alba:

Email: info@focusonsolution.com

Phone: 248-946-4702

Website: www.focusonsolution.com

LinkedIn: linkedin.com/in/albaconrod

Facebook: https://www.facebook.com/focusonsolution.fons
Instagram: https://www.instagram.com/focusonsolution.fons/

---

1 Robert B. Kaiser and Darren V. Overfield, "Strengths, strengths overused, and lopsided leadership," *Consulting Psychology Journal: Practice and Research* 63, no. 2 (June 2011): 89–109, doi.org/10.1037/a0024470

2 Brené Brown, Ph.D., L.M.S.W, *The Gifts of Imperfection: Let Go of Who You Think You Are Supposed to Be and Embrace Who You Are* (Minnesota: Hazelden, 2010), 56–57.

3 Brown, *The Gifts of Imperfection*, 57.

Andrew Franseen

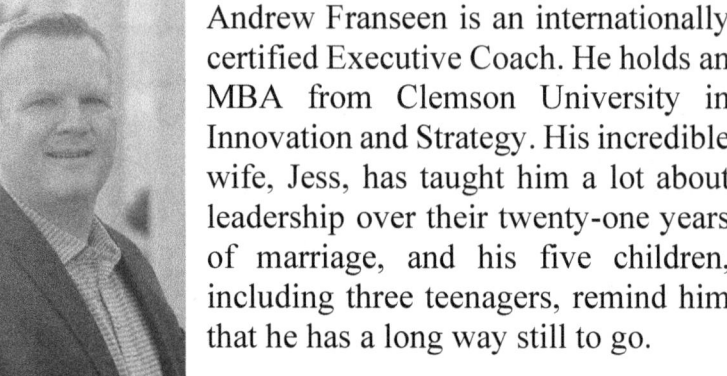

Andrew Franseen is an internationally certified Executive Coach. He holds an MBA from Clemson University in Innovation and Strategy. His incredible wife, Jess, has taught him a lot about leadership over their twenty-one years of marriage, and his five children, including three teenagers, remind him that he has a long way still to go.

Andrew helps companies accelerate their leadership pipeline by providing executive coaching that is contextualized to each client and each company. He likes to say that the real business he is in is the ultimate business of human flourishing. Leaders do not have to lose their humanity in order to lead effectively, indeed the very best leaders keep human dignity, respect, and professionalism at the heart of their leadership.

Andrew cheers for his Kansas City Chiefs and Clemson Tigers and his kid's lacrosse, track, golf, and basketball teams. He especially enjoys coaching clients on the golf course.

The Craft of Conflict
Do to others as you would like them to do to you. -Jesus

By Andrew Franseen

Cracking your success code demands partnerships. You don't choose that path. Even for the self-employed solopreneur, you will need strategic partners and, at some point, at least one customer.

Where there are relationships, there will be conflict. This chapter invites you to consider conflict itself as a craft to be mastered.

Fear not; this is not an invitation to soft skills. Indeed, I'm on a mission to eliminate soft skills. Or more specifically, to rebrand soft skills into the "harder skills" that they truly are. If "soft skills" was a marketing technique of some social sciences department somewhere, it alienated its target customer right out of the gate and should go down as one of the worst branding exercises of all time. (Turns out, "soft virtues" go back centuries to a world far away from my American context.)

I've never met anyone who says, "I want to get softer." Not one. Ever.

Most of my clients are highly successful men. Men's men. More gladiators than genteel gentlemen. One client looked at me with deeply skeptical eyes as we talked about what his communication approach was costing him, and he accused me of "trying to make [him] soft," as if I were engaging in high crimes.

"Soft? No," I volleyed back, "human, professional, classy. That is my goal." This was clearly a new way of looking at diplomacy and tact for him, but he was far from sold.

The craft of conflict, as laid out below, is an invitation for exceptionally smart and highly successful leaders, both men and women, both professionally educated and personally educated. It is for white collar and blue and clerical and green. It's an invitation to a herculean endeavor that will not only help you crack your success code, but it will safeguard you from sabotaging your success.

Culture is King now more than ever

Seth Godin's simple definition of culture is one I give him credit for regularly in my coaching. Culture simply pinpoints that "people like us do things like this." Too many great leaders still think that culture is about being buddies, buying ping-pong tables for Gen Zers, or doing the latest rendition of a trust fall. All of that is more coddling than culture, or it may very well be a culture of coddling.

Culture is inevitable and inescapable

When Deon Sanders took over as head coach of the University of Colorado football team, he made it clear to the current roster and scholarship athletes that they would likely want to transfer because he has a highly disciplined winning formula. The Buffaloes had just gone 4-8. Forty-one players entered the transfer portal. The portal, though understandable, is in many ways the latest disruptive gimmick that caters to teenage disquiet.

So, when Coach Prime, Deon's favorite name for himself, was asked about this new culture that he was bringing, he rebuked the reporter. "I don't care about culture." The highly decorated and even more highly bejeweled coach shot back. From behind the sunglasses, he went on, "I don't even care if they like each other, man. I want to win. I've been on some teams where the quarterback doesn't like the receiver, but they sure made harmony when the ball was snapped." Deon was a receiver in the NFL. But I must ask, is it about "making harmony" or just winning?

Deon, like way too many leaders, thinks that talking about "culture" is about being soft, being buddies, hanging out, and liking each other. While it is preferable to like each other rather than despise your colleagues, I get the criticism. And it is fair. "Culture" means everything, and therefore it means precious little, except something like "soft" and "friends." The word itself has not really graduated into professional circles, even though plenty of Fortune 500 companies have HR professionals focused on their culture.

"Culture" is way more inclusive than just the nature of our relationships, though, I would argue, never less than that. But more importantly, your organization, your non-profit, and your team has a culture. Period. It's inevitable and inescapable. Sadly, too many times the culture is just the personality of the strongest person writ large. If she is highly analytical and forceful, the culture of the team will shade that way. If he operates and executes at a more rapid—even schizophrenic— pace, the entire organization will value efficiency and speed and will tend to sacrifice discernment, strategy, and communication.

Edgar Schein, an authority on organizational culture, taught that the personality of the owner of a company practically *determines* the culture of the organization. In geographically dispersed companies and teams, cultures can take on much more of their own flavor, which makes culture clarity all the more important if, for instance, you want your sales professional four states away to "represent the brand accurately and compellingly."

Since culture is inevitable and inescapable, the best course forward is to define it. Codify the culture. Call them vision and values. Call them Priorities and Philosophy and Policies. Call them whatever you want. Have three, thirteen, or thirty. At the heart of the matter is always this question: What people will we be and what will we prioritize? For instance, do we believe that every person in our organization is a noble person of infinite dignity, even on their worst days? Or do we believe that the people in the lowest blocks of the organizational chart, the ones out there on the front line, the newbies on the manufacturing line, are more like tools than people with aspirations? Are they cheap? Most of them will be gone within six months. They are a dime-a-dozen. That philosophy will determine your culture and especially your leadership culture.

Culture is about humanity and dignity

One of my clients is in the insurance industry. His agents are professionals and do excellent work. He is a rock star, patiently and methodically shooting for the moon. One brand that he represents invited him to a niche meeting with the president of the company. The president went on and on about the values that she is driving through the company, one of which is "the golden rule." It's a multi-billion-dollar brand with no religious affiliations. Indeed, the owner is outspokenly anti-religion. The golden rule is simply about how we treat each other, whether team members, people above or below us on the organizational chart, our strategic partners, our customers, or even our complainers, the ones that leave impossibly embarrassing reviews on the world wide web.

One of my colleagues told me that there is a new rule that is better than the golden rule. She said, "It's the platinum rule." I responded with intense curiosity, "It's hard to do better than the Rabbi Jesus and a rule that has stood for 2,000 years but let me in on this new rule." She went on, "The platinum rule just says to treat others the way *they* want to be treated." She thought the golden rule was saying to use your own categories of what you want and then do that for others whether that is what they need or not. It's an honest misunderstanding of the original proverb.

In the Gospel of Luke, when Jesus is teaching this as a really core teaching to his followers, he is defining their culture. Most specifically, he defines the culture for when they are in conflict. He is literally answering the question: how should we treat those who hate us, those who consider us their enemies, those who cuss us up one side and down the other, those who hurt us, and those who mistreat us?

In those circumstances, Jesus insisted, be these kinds of people. Be people who do good to others. Although their treatment of you may be dehumanizing, how do you wish to be treated? Well treat them with full humanity and dignity. This is no justification for abuse and surely not a mantra for pacificism in the workplace. It's an invitation into a certain conflict culture.

Whether you like the ancient Rabbi or not is beside the point here. Culture answers the question, "What people will we be?" That builds out of how we see others. This is more fundamental than any DEI initiative could ever be. You don't have to be interested in Jesus in the least to recognize, like the president of that national brand, that the golden rule is still good for business. Studies are increasingly showing that without a baseline of trust, good faith, and basic human dignity, DEI initiatives will be unsuccessful and potentially detrimental. They will lock polarization into a company or campus more than they will till the soil and nurture a fruitful field with a healthy ecosystem.

Your Conflict is Your Culture

When defining your culture, you might address your values around innovation, pace, response times, safety, customers, revenue, leadership, training, and so much more.

But most consequential for your culture is how your conflict looks and feels. Take that in. I can tell most about a team or a company by how its conflict looks and feels. For some, conflict is nonexistent. Harmony, albeit superficial, stands as the ultimate. For some, aggression is everywhere. Competitiveness is the norm. Winning is everything. (Deon accidentally defined the number one point of his culture while he was dismissing culture: "I want to win.")

For some teams, the conflict is always one-way. Always down. The leader pushes down directives, and whether the subordinates agree or disagree or have something useful to add remains irrelevant. Patrick Lencioni, in his *Five Dysfunctions of a Team* shows why this approach is such a waste of money as employees become more and more disengaged, mindless workers looking forward to clocking out, searching for other companies on LinkedIn, and ultimately retirement. If a leader wants to awaken her workforce, she creates high-functioning conflict around their shared future.

Ultimately, leaders embody the actual culture of a team or company, regardless of what values are listed on the website or the lobby walls. When leaders carefully craft meetings and interpersonal interactions to artfully expose substantive differences that improve results and better the team, then leaders not only engage their workforce at deeper, more emotional levels, but they also exude a culture of high-functioning, constructive conflict. The environment becomes one where conflict is compelling and inviting to even the most shy and reserved team member, the one who fears disagreeing with his superior because of management wounds from his last employer.

Many times, when companies or teams get toxic, the sole culprit is the nature of their conflict. In a toxic culture, people can be disrespectful and even dehumanizing. I find this fascinating, especially in manufacturing environments. Manufacturing can easily dehumanize simply by its monotony. The monotony conditions people to turn their minds off. I live ten minutes from the biggest BMW plant in North America and have friends all through the organization. BMW, like others, works hard to change things up for their line-workers, not only for physiological reasons but also psychological. Their mental muscles of creativity, problem-solving, and ambition weaken.

But here is where it really gets interesting. These same workers who are so crucial to delivering an exceptional product are assigned a line-leader who further "motivates" with insults and threats. There is no more perfect formula for high turnover, especially among the best employees. There is no surer path to safety problems. The dysfunctional conflict in some of these plants is systemic and generational. The plant operator himself started on that line and was treated like a tool.

Four Dysfunctional Cultures

Dysfunctional cultures abound. Results can still be delivered in dysfunctional cultures, but better, faster, and less costly results will be delivered in high-functioning cultures. If your conflict is your culture, consider these four types of dysfunctional cultures.

Passive-aggressive. The passive-aggressive culture arises naturally from passive-aggressive leaders whose primary skill is to move people through indirect methods. To put this in Seth Godin's terminology, People like us do things like indirect wording through indirect methods. We employ the silent treatment, subtle rumor spreading, and worse. The answer to passive-aggressive cultures is high-functioning conflict, where direct communication is expected and even safeguarded.

Passive-passive. Have you seen the passive-passive culture? It's overly self-effacing. People like us apologize for any self-expression that slips through the tightly guarded walls. It's a culture that is excessively submissive. People like us are doormats. This is the harmony-at-all-cost culture. These leaders do not resort to indirect communication; they stick with no communication at all. When a senior leader is hyper-aggressive, this is the most natural outcome for his team.

Aggressive-passive. Then there is the aggressive-passive, where leaders lead with an edge only to realize that they have done more damage than necessary, so they become conciliatory. I mean, they do not ask for forgiveness for shredding a worker, but they are willing to show sheepishness and a little regret. But the next disagreement will feel the same way.

Aggressive-aggressive. Finally, there is the aggressive-aggressive culture, where everyone is direct virtually all the time. Well, not everyone! The people with the most power are the most direct. They speak over, interrupt, dismiss, and belittle others. Sometimes this is unknowing because they have been in power so long and so many people have allowed them to get away with it. It's not that they have mastered the skill of escalation; escalation is all they have ever known. They have two communication tools: the wrench and the sledgehammer.

Often, it's how they were treated by their parents, coach, mentor, or manager. It's become their heart-language. People like us are large and threatening. The worst thing about the aggressive-aggressive culture is that each layer of leadership gets away with it from those below. If the CEO is aggressive-aggressive, he tacitly permits his lieutenants to adopt that mindset and treat people below them the same way.

Considerateness Transforms Conflict

I won't go soft on you if you don't go soft on me!

In our hyper-paced work cultures, conflict easily becomes dysfunctional, destructive, and ultimately costly to both results and relationships. We budget very little time for meaningful debate, we feel rushed to make a decision, and often we don't really care about the other people in the conflict.

Put simply, we are inconsiderate.

Considerateness is the craft of high-functioning, productive, innovative, revenue-generating, cost-saving conflict.

Considerateness is what makes conflict professional, respectful, and classy. Considerateness makes a company more compelling to potential employees and sets the standard for how we will work with our customers. People like us do things like being considerate in conflict.

There is nothing soft about this skill. It's a craft. It requires herculean discipline, brilliant strategic planning, and incredible self-restraint.

By considerate, I do not intend excessively quiet, passive, and so gentle as to never get your point across. Considerateness takes the best of the passive-passive culture—staying quiet—but transforms that into active listening that is artful, curious, and constructive.

By considerate, I do not intend *softspokenness* that always dials down emotions and word choice to not possibly offend anyone ever.

Considerate is about tone and words, but it is first and foremost about mindset. Being considerate transforms combative into collegial, criticism into collaboration, and cutting confrontation into constructiveness.

And that is not easy. There is nothing soft. One must muster courage and bravery to truly be considerate. One must remain disciplined, focused, and curious. But above all, one must check his or her ego at the door. Considerateness happens when humility is coupled with commitment to the mission and the person.

Crafting Considerateness

At the core of considerateness is "to consider." Considerateness is so much more than tone, emotion, or word choice. It's an attitude. It's an attitude of curiosity. It's an attitude that looks at other people as basically smart with something important to contribute. Here is how you can craft considerateness into your conflict.

Know Thyself. Humans are still better at self-deception than self-awareness. We see ourselves more out of our aspirations and wishes than out of a long look in an actual mirror with the proper light exposing the full picture. I lead clients on a journey to *general* self-awareness that can come from assessments like DISC, Predictive Index, or Strengths Finder. In addition, I like to press clients toward more specific self-awareness that considers their aspirations, their career path, their family status, their stress points, their leadership experiences, and more.

But there is nothing more powerful for self-awareness than 360-degree, developmental, *non-anonymous* feedback. I told you there was nothing soft about this. If you want to test the strength of your team, particularly their trust in each other, arrange for this feedback. I advise a group session where everyone gets 45 minutes to an hour in the hotseat. Let the CEO go first. Each person leads out with a self-assessment that is role-specific but also deeply personal. After about 15-20 minutes of this, the team members add their assessment, building on what was said and, at times, challenging the self-assessment. A facilitator can help, particularly early on when deploying this tool for the first time. A facilitator will provide safety and keep it constructive. The key to making these times highly productive is to frame them as development. If it is simply feedback, then the time can become more destructive. If you set it up under the reality that none of us have arrived and that all of us want to grow, then we can absorb the insight as a gift rather than a simmering slight finally given a moment to erupt.

Many leaders that I work with want honest feedback. They muster enough courage to constrain their egos and they pursue critical, constructive insight. But few colleagues will provide it. If they will not provide it, then one of two problems is usually present: either the leader has created a culture of destructive conflict, or the teammate does not want to open him or herself up to critical feedback from others. The leader may have to make a declaration that there can be no retribution based on honest feedback. The leader may also need to issue a *mea culpa* for creating a passive-passive culture because of his aggressiveness.

Know the Other. Many of us tend not only to be overly optimistic toward ourselves, even if we have learned how to couch it all in apparent modesty, but we also tend to be overly hard on others. Our expectations for them are high, sometimes impossibly high. We just wish they thought, moved, talked, and prioritized just like me. I've heard too many leaders spell out detailed explanations for slumping revenue, and it's all just a professional blame shift. They might love the idea of *Extreme Ownership*, but they feel they have arrived at this while others still have plenty of progress to make. I have also witnessed leaders take ownership of failures three or four layers down the organizational chart. I've wondered, "How in the world can you possibly take ownership for that failure?" But it was his team. He was responsible.

When I provide a DISC debrief to my client, we spend about half the time on himself and how others likely perceive him. But then we take a look at her team, and I exhort the leader to study her team, their emotions, and their preferred communication approach.

Slow down to be more efficient. Leaders often express to me in some way or another that we just don't have time for what feels to them like pedantic, overly relational conflict. These same leaders have also never taken the time to count the cost of their rushed, dysfunctional conflict. Hyper-efficient managers rarely do an autopsy on the failures that arise from their hurried decisions. There just isn't enough time for that!

Hurried hires not only increase turnover but also undermine credibility. CEOs are notoriously bad at hiring, yet they oftentimes believe they are prescient in picking talent. These same people look at two rockstars that are driving results in the company and take quick ownership for those hires, but they have long forgotten the eight high-potential hires who lasted less than a year.

If your urgency is off the charts, then start your day with a run or exhausting workout. Please stop the habit of starting the day with an energy drink! Pace yourself as a discipline. Your team (and your family) will appreciate it. High-quality decisions are rarely rushed. And if the decision ought to be a team decision, then you are going to have to slow way down for a more effective outcome. But it's not just more effective. While it pains you to sit still that long, it is far more efficient than rushing a poor or mediocre decision.

Sure, some leaders need to pick up the pace, but most need to count the cost of running so fast. The cost includes the physical and emotional health of the leader himself. Many leaders are so engaged in the business and the hunt that they accidentally detach from the most meaningful relationships. They also detach from their own well-being. Companies deserve to be led by healthy leaders. As I said in the introduction, this chapter on considerateness in conflict will help safeguard you from sabotaging your own success.

Being quiet and listening are not the same thing. As you slow down, you slow down to ask perceptive questions and to dialogue around critical decisions. But being quiet and letting others talk is not the same thing as active and artful listening. Steven Sample in *The Contrarian's Guide to Leadership* calls for artful listening that remains open, non-defensive, and curious. An active listener continues to ask clarifying questions and doesn't mind if someone in the room thinks she should already know the answer to that. Stephen Covey invited us to "Seek first to understand, then to be understood." With our shrinking attention spans, perhaps nothing has suffered more than the art of listening well.

Has it ever been your experience as you observe a conversation or a conflict where you think to yourself, "He clearly did not listen to what she just said?" Someone goes off on a tangent that confuses everyone, or answers a question that was never asked, or interjects without allowing the person to even finish the thought. Too many conversations are not conversations at all but multiple people talking to, or sometimes at, each other.

The best listeners keep a pen and paper to track the conversation and key insights. These tools are so much more effective than a computer, which is sure to distract even the most focused officer. If you must digitize, simply snap a picture of the notes and file it on your device.

Candor is seen most clearly in questions. What questions are allowed to be asked? How will they be asked? How deep can we press into problems and opportunities? The leaders who lead best master the power of questions. Questions not only make people feel good, like you value their input, but more importantly, questions engage and awaken the creativity in your team like little else. If you want a great meeting, take fifteen minutes to craft a great question.

Sadly, many leaders can't handle questions because they are so used to being the boss and dictating the actions that they lose a measure of control by asking a question. By asking a question, you acknowledge that other people bring experiences, perspectives, and especially competencies to the matter that you lack. You can always command, but can you collaborate in a constructive and creative way?

Questions set you up to consider and be considerate of valuable input from your team. Sure, some will offer less-than-helpful responses at times. But you can sift through those easily. Don't grow impatient. Efficiency is not your friend when aiming for high-insight decisions.

Remaining moderate requires greater courage. I want to say it again and again; there is just nothing soft about this. Being harsh and severe is weak, lacking self-restraint. The high-functioning conflict that I'm describing can be psychologically exhausting and extremely hard work. It takes hard work to hold your first reaction and listen for an entire thought. It demands intensity and focus to think through the nuances. It invites courage coupled with modesty to disagree while identifying key points of agreement.

Hard skills and Harder ones

This whole conversation reminds me of a teacher I had in middle school who went off on me about how easy the game of golf was. I mean, the ball just sits there. Nothing like baseball or tennis. I said, "Go ahead. Give it your best shot. I bet you can't even hit the ball, let alone hit it only four times to get it in the hole 400 yards away. Go ahead." I don't know if he ever did it, but I remember the feeling of shock that a person who has never tried the sport was certain that it was so easy.

Same with considerateness in the craft of conflict.

Could you be dismissing, even demeaning, the very idea simply because you don't want to fail? Instead, apply your competitiveness to this. See how many times in an hour-long meeting you can resist speaking. See how many creative, eye-opening questions you can offer. Count how many times you can go out of your way to identify points of agreement for the team. Take note of the engagement levels of all the other participants. Make it your ambition to increase engagement of your most timid teammate. Celebrate with the team when tensions rise but temperatures remain cool. Now, do even better next time.

***

To contact Andrew:

Text: 864-380-3612

andrewfranseen.com

Deborah Kaler

Deborah Kaler has been in Christian ministry for over 30 years and holds certificates in Biblical Counseling Programs.

Deborah has gracefully walked through addiction, depression, and adultery and wore the "Scarlet Letter of Divorce." During her healing journey, she watched God miraculously heal her marriage and put it back together again! God has done miracle after miracle in her life, through the good and the bad!

Her story is one of God's faithfulness, grace, restoration, redemption, and LOVE! Her heart is to help hurting, broken women, full of guilt and shame, see themselves as the Beautiful Diamond they are, hear God's voice, and become whole.

Deborah teaches, coaches & does speaking engagements for women who have experienced similar situations. She teaches them to see themselves the way God sees them, as Precious and a Beautiful Diamond!

"Instead of your shame, you shall receive a double portion, and instead of disgrace, you will rejoice in your inheritance. And so, you will inherit a double portion in your land and everlasting joy will be yours!" Isaiah 61:7

Dare To Hope Again!

By Deborah Kaler

I want you to know that no matter where you are in your walk with God, no matter what you've done AFTER coming to Jesus, however much guilt and shame you are carrying CANNOT stop the LOVE that God has for you and the call on your life. He has an awesome plan for you, and there is a wonderful purpose for why you are alive for such a time as this!

Many years ago, in 1991, God gave me a vision, in a ladies' Bible study, of a HUGE plain gray rock. It was the size of a boulder. I asked the Lord what it meant, and He said nothing. I just kept staring at it. As the leader began to close in prayer, the picture changed, and the plain gray rock suddenly turned into the most beautiful, colorful, multifaceted, huge, sparkling DIAMOND I had ever seen! God then told me, "Deborah, you see yourself as a plain gray rock, but I see you as a Beautiful Diamond!!!" Revelation 21:18,19: "In New Jerusalem, the walls are made of jasper (diamonds) and the city of pure gold, as pure as glass. The foundations of the city were decorated with every kind of precious stone. The first foundation was Jasper."

There was also another vision given to me during that time. It was a picture of a massive tree with its arms spread out. It was like a giant Sequoia with many smaller trees below. It was like the larger tree was protecting the smaller ones. Satan had a rope tied around the Sequoia and was trying to pull it down, though he couldn't because the roots were too deep. The following picture was of the same tree with the same rope the enemy had tried to pull it down with, and it was now turned into a swing with a little girl swinging on it. The Lord showed me that what the enemy meant for harm, God was going to use for good. In Genesis 50:20, the Bible says, "As for you, you thought evil against me; that God meant it for good, to bring to pass as it is this day to save many people."

I shared this vision with my friend Cathy in 1998, and she got all excited and said that she had something for me. She gave me a poster that had a picture of God's fingers holding a rope that was a rope swing with a little girl swinging on it! The poster said, "Do you trust Me?" Oh my gosh, I got so excited and asked her where she got this. She told me she was in Walmart, and a man just walked up to her, handed it to her, and then walked away. I believe that was an Angel! God continually asked me, "Do you trust me?"

Several months later, in January of 1992, something very traumatic happened to me, and I literally watched my mind unwind while standing in my living room. I had my 3rd child at the end of that year, and within three months, I was completely non-functional. A Doctor diagnosed and treated me for severe bipolar depression, and one of the medicines she prescribed for me made me very ill, so I couldn't take it, and I just got worse and worse. I couldn't pack a lunch or clean a toilet. I also got my life's dream of owning a horse that year. I couldn't walk out to the barn and give her a carrot and some love, let alone go out to groom her and ride her! I would just stand at the back window and bawl and bawl. I was in bed for five years and would just lay in my bed, cry, and sleep. All the while asking, "What is wrong with me?"

God is so faithful. He truly never left my side! He continually ministered to me about the call and purpose He had for my life. I was to minister to the "hurting women in the body of Christ." He told me how much He loved me and the call on my life to "tell them I love them." He gave me dreams and visions, and I read my Bible, with which He spoke. He was so loving and kind, full of grace and mercy, and gave me so many promises of the future of me sharing my testimony with the world. His voice was crystal clear… "Do you trust me?" He never stopped ministering to me His Love and His Word. He promised to do everything He showed me in His time and His way.

One of the things He told me was that I would minister to hurting women in the body of Christ who were full of guilt and shame to help them see themselves as the Beautiful Diamonds they really are, hear God's voice, and become whole. He showed me on stages with liquid gold being poured into me.

My 10-year-old daughter was caring for my newborn baby and my 5-year-old son. My husband worked a lot of overtime and commuted 3 hours a day. He didn't understand what was wrong with me. He concluded that I must be taking and abusing drugs, which I wasn't. He had to start doing many things in the house that he had not done before. My home fell apart as I could not keep it up, which added to my depression. My husband got angrier and angrier with each day, month, and year that I was in bed.

I had surgery in September 1995. Something went desperately wrong, and I was left in excruciating pain. I was prescribed large doses of Vicodin for six months. I not only felt better physically, but I also felt better emotionally. It helped take away some of the pressure of not being me and the pain of not being able to function as a wife and Mom. I was now thoroughly addicted to the medicine and was very suicidal. I had lost all hope of getting better and my family healing. Watching my family and home deteriorate daily was so painful, compounding my agony. I continually cried out to God, and He always answered, asking me the same question: "Do you trust me?" I did trust Him and knew that, somehow, He would bring good out of this all.

In August of 1996, I went to a Rodney Howard Brown Crusade. God touched me there in a compelling way. When Paula White prayed for me, I fell backward, and suddenly, I was taken into a vision. Instantly, I was in Heaven on a gurney with a doctor on my left, one at my head, and one on my right. They had scrubs on from head to toe, including masks, so that I couldn't see their faces. The doctor on my right reached into my chest and pulled out a small white stone in place of my heart. With the stone in the palm of His left hand, he turned and passed his hand through a flame, and the white stone was instantly turned into a big red beating heart! I asked him to please put it back in my chest! It had been so many years since I had been well. Instead, I saw myself on my bed, in my bedroom back on earth, and someone was shutting my door with a cat-like face that was hissing. I heard God speaking, "you have no place here". He was speaking to Satan. Then suddenly, I was back in Heaven asking the doctor to please put my heart back in my chest. The next thing I knew, I was back in my bedroom again. I was laying on my back, on my floor, in my bedroom with an Angel standing on each side of me with their swords crossed over me, and again I heard God speak to Satan." You cannot have her, she is mine!" Once, again, I was in Heaven asking for my heart to be put back in me and before I could finish talking the doctor on my left reached into his chest and pulled his heart out and put it in my chest and instantly my chest was healed, with no scarring Then I was back on earth again and I was standing on a stage. I was facing the audience, but it was dark out there, and I couldn't see who I was speaking to. He revealed to me that the doctor on my right was the Holy Spirit, the doctor at my head was the Father, and the doctor to my left was Jesus! Ezekiel 36:26: "A new heart also will I give you, and a new spirit will I put within you: and I will take away the stony heart out of your flesh, and I will give you a heart of flesh."

I also went to a Joyce Meyer conference during that time. God had shown me a picture of, like looking into a tunnel and seeing a light far off, and He told me that the end was coming about six months before her conference. While there, He showed me a picture of a huge mountain with a hole on the side and me coming out of the tunnel into the sunlight ("Son light"). Oh my gosh, the sun was warm, and I felt so wonderful and free! There was a river coming out of the mountain, and it ran gently down with trees on each side of it. I saw myself under one of those trees down the way with my horse, Babe, and my German shepherd, Jake. I asked the Lord if I was going to be able to ride Babe again because it had been so many years, and he zoomed in on the picture where she was standing right beside me with her bridle and saddle on her. I got so excited!!!

By now, my drug use was now totally out of control. My husband put me into a 30-day dual diagnosis program for depression and addiction. It was a live-in program, and the first night there, a man approached me and looked at me like I was the most beautiful woman alive. I was starved for attention, so I decided to receive his advances. I told God that I was going to see this man when I got out of the program and that Jesus couldn't come with me. So, I walked away from Jesus and started using drugs again because I couldn't live without Him and tried to numb the pain.

One evening, in his home, God showed up and told me that "even though I thought I had walked away from Him, he had not left me." He said, "Right here, right now, you are my Beautiful Diamond!" He said I didn't have to be 'doing' something like teaching, leading worship, 'being good' or 'perfect.' That He loved me just like I was! That I couldn't earn His love because it is a free gift. That He knew me (completely) and loved me (anyway)! That totally blew my mind! He said that He doesn't so much look at what I'm doing, but He looks at my heart and why I am doing what I am doing! Fully known and fully loved!

I went to a new Doctor and told him I didn't know who I was. When I looked in the mirror, all I could see were wrinkles on my face, and there were wrinkles on my hands, and I wondered where the last five years had gone! It was like God had brought me back to life again!!! He also restored my reasoning in an instant! I didn't even know it was gone. He is so big and so faithful!

I didn't have a dad growing up, and it crippled me emotionally. "If my own Dad doesn't love me, who could?" This was my mantra growing up. I was very promiscuous and craved male attention. I started doing drugs when I was 14, had an abortion at 15, and was sticking needles in my arms at 19. I was with a guy who beat me, and I felt like I deserved it because I had such hatred toward myself. I was afraid if somebody found out who I really was, then they, too, would hate me, so I had to keep my distance from everyone. I never felt safe, even when I was young.

God had revealed to me that I was shame-based and that my grandpa had sexually abused me when I was just a little girl. He showed me that was one reason I hated myself. I blamed myself for the abuse, which is why I saw myself as unlovable. I had no remembrance of the abuse, but it still affected me in a very negative way. No wonder I never felt safe. I also had a spirit of abandonment and rejection on me.

In the Bible, Luke:15, verses 4-7, tells the story of a man with 100 sheep. "If he loses one of them, does he not leave the ninety-nine in the wilderness and go after the lost until he finds it? And when he has found it, he lays it on his shoulders, rejoicing. And when he comes home, he calls together his friends and neighbors, saying to them, rejoice with me; for I have found my sheep which was lost. I say to you that likewise joy shall be in Heaven over one sinner that repents, more than over ninety- nine just persons, which need no repentance."

I am like that one lost sheep, and Jesus came and found me and brought me back home, literally! My husband and I divorced and remarried two years later! I would love to tell you that we lived happily ever after…Not! Instead, we have worked through many different issues through the years and love each other very much. We are very thankful that God chose to put us back together! My husband had to ask God for a new heart; the old one had been through too much, so God did! I'm so thankful I'm married to a godly man who prays and listens! We have been married 41 years and have three children and two grandchildren! Only God!

God has always been a God of miracles to me. As a brand-new Christian, he healed my German Shepherd when my neighbor kicked her and poisoned her with antifreeze. She was bleeding internally, and her liver had shut down. The vet told me to take her home to die. Instead, God gave her a brand-new liver! Her numbers came back up, and the Dr. said it was a miracle. She lived five more years! He also gave my Great Dane a brand-new spine! UC Davis didn't know what happened but that it would continue to deteriorate, and she would die. Like my Linka, Brandi got better and lived a full life, and they said it was a miracle!

In October 2020, I was diagnosed with lung cancer. The doctors ordered all the tests, and when I went in for the biopsy in November, the doctor decided not to do the test because something else was happening in my lung. There was a white substance there besides the cancer. He didn't know what it was, and he even showed me the pictures of the scan. I knew it was God doing something miraculous! When they rechecked it on December 19, my lung was completely clear! I was so thankful, blessed, and overwhelmed by His grace and goodness in my life! What a wonderful Christmas present!

This is my story. Now, let's talk about you. Are you lonely? Do you feel worthless? Do you have addictions or a physical or mental illness? Does life have no meaning, no purpose? How about self-hatred or hopelessness, loneliness or isolation? Do you need hope?

God knows your problems and is way bigger than any problem you may have or any situation you may be in. He knows you better than you know yourself. He knit you together in your mother's womb. He knows the number of hairs on your head. You are Jesus' Bride!

He takes our sins and throws them into the Sea of Forgetfulness, never to be remembered again. If we ask Him to forgive us again, He says, "what sin?". It is completely gone. That is why Jesus went to the cross. He took all our sins away, past, present, and future. He died and rose again so that we could have an abundant life with no guilt or shame.

He wants you to learn how to receive His love. He has an awesome plan for your life! He just wants you to come to Him, just like you are. So many people feel that they have out-sinned God, whether they are Christians or not. That is one of the enemy's greatest tools. God's love is greater than any sin. He wants you to know who He is and His amazing, unchangeable love for you.

***

To contact Deborah:

Cell: 707 761-0702

Email: Elitediamonds7@gmail.com

Suzanne Sullivan

Lady Suzanne is a speaker, trainer, coach and writer, who loves to inspire personal, professional, or business growth. Let's Design YR Destiny!

Suzanne and Paul, her husband of over 50 years, are blessed with three children, and ten grand-girls. She loves being a Guiding Grandma, her bi-coastal life and making a difference. She is an adventurer who has never met a stranger and owns a small property in Scotland. Her guiding principles are Faith, Family, Finances, Fueling Health, Fun, Friends, and Future legacy. 'Have bag packed - will travel', is one of her mottoes, along with "Living the Dream" and "Blessed".

Her motto: 'If I can, you can too', break through challenges to fulfill your dreams and become a winner!"

A sled dog ride at Christmas inspired 'Lightning Leadership'. The amazing lead dog knew his role, as the dog team precisely performed the Musher's commands. An exhilarating ride as the wide fans of snow sprayed off the rails. Join Lady Suzanne on a journey to crack the code for success.

Lightening Leadership – The Secret Code is 360
A Blueprint for Harnessing Leadership, from behind!

By Suzanne Sullivan

LEAD YOURSELF FIRST, THEN INSPIRE THE TEAM.

Lessons learned from the Iditarod Sled Dog Race. Become a winner!

'**Lightning,**' the lead dog for an Alaskan Dog Sled Team, earned his position due to his innate desire to run fast, his endurance and ability to synchronize the team's pace. The team leader, or Musher, as a human, possesses unique problem-solving, analytical, and visionary skills to design and execute one of the ultimate sports. Lightning's intuition and intelligence, though remarkable, required the Mushers' guidance and instructions, from the back sled rails, for a winning team.

WHY LEADERSHIP: GROWTH TO GREATNESS

Leadership skills are desirable because they create a positive impact for self and others, and as goals are achieved, the opportunities expand for increased success and satisfaction. Leveraging achievements, including increasing income, becomes a foundation for ongoing personal and professional development to fulfill a sense of purpose and gain respect.

Leadership is a work ethic, nurtured and desired, empowering individuals to take charge of their lives, and fosters personal and professional growth. Fine-tuning yourself creates an edge over others who have no direction. Before a crisis occurs, a leader's awareness will keep the cogs in the progress-wheel from jamming.

Success breeds confidence, a growth mindset and momentum forward, even when dealing with the trials of each day. One should seek to grow skills with a focus on creating positive impacts, fostering collaboration, and contributing to the overall well-being of individuals and communities.

"You are never too old to set another goal or to dream a new dream." C.S. Lewis

Deciding your purpose, marks the beginning of change. Explore, find, and create a new YOU. Embracing change influences your thinking and mindset choices. Seize the day to create a better future. **See it-believe it- do it!**

Leadership is dynamic extending beyond a title and is a way of fulfilling a vision with an unseen destination. However, the journey is not without challenges. Overcoming a myriad of obstacles builds strength, confidence, and insights for improvement. Guiding a team to the finish takes focus to sustain the journey and viewing 360° creates synergy.

"It always seems impossible until it's done." Nelson Mandela

While there's no magic pill, there is magic in working on leadership for self-improvement, expanding your thinking, and achieving your goals. Developing skills builds confidence and self-worth has value, even if responsibilities increase.

Self-made leaders take responsibility for decisions, adapt as needed, and persevere in the direction of their dreams. Plus, they engage in reasoning, make decisions evaluating the long-term impact, use integrity and walk their talk. They eliminate procrastination, self-centeredness, lack of empathy, negativity, and failure to reassess plans.

A great leader is a person of integrity gifted with 360° insights into how decisions will impact all. They control their emotions, think logically, and design a clear roadmap forward; they are not defined by their past, doubts, fear, feelings of worthlessness and 'I was meant for more.'

Water your desire for growth as it sprouts and realize all change requires commitment, understanding of the task, patience, practice, and planning. Positivity pays dividends!

"360° Analyzing increases insights to success in your life!", Lady Suzanne

Being aware of 360° around you to maintain efficiency, effectiveness, and enhancement!

GOALS

Choose to be a Musher with SMART goals and positive determination. Clear internal confusion and focus forward only. Be a go-getter, goal-oriented and gallant. Also, be like Lightning, always happy and ready to run!

Goals are concrete decisions of a desired result or change. It is mentally freeing to create lists, cross off tasks, and create steps for achievement! Bonuses are organization, timeliness, and progress.

"Setting a goal is not the main thing. *It is deciding how you will go about achieving it and staying with that plan."* Tom Landry

Success stories begin with planting the seed of a sharp VISION, crafting a detailed DESIGN, training a capable

TEAM, embracing a shared MISSION, and nurturing unwavering FAITH in the PLAN.

After designing the dream on paper, learn the skills, build a support team, and go forth. Don't quit your daydreams. Rest if you must, regroup but don't give up on something you think about daily or weekly. Progress is not always straightforward; the fog must clear.

"Never begin the day until it is finished on paper." Jim Rohn

If some goals seem out of reach or perplexing, choose short-term doable goals, and grow them. It takes stepping out of your comfort zone, turning off the negative replay loops in the mind and becoming thick-skinned. If you want to create positive impact and be influential, then create self-leadership.

"By failing to prepare, you are preparing to fail." Benjamin Franklin

DESTINATION *"It takes as much energy to wish as it does to plan."* — Eleanor Roosevelt

Ships were never designed to stay docked in a harbor, and neither are you! Our lives are full of options and opportunities. Leave your comfort zone, get unstuck, go, and look for your destiny. Yes, there will be unexpected storms, delays, and roadblocks, but don't give up. Instead find alternatives.

I personally think about leadership, as **LEADING-MY-SHIP.** Success occurs when your vision is measurable and attainable, steps are planned, and a line is drawn to the destination.

See it, believe it, achieve it!

Turning the small rudder a few degrees on a huge ship will take it to another destination. Adjust your rudder frequently to fulfill your vision and purpose. Gain an updated version of inner software to create a new YOU. Search, seek, discover, and enjoy the journey.

"I have been impressed with the urgency of doing. Knowing is not enough;

we must apply. Being willing is not enough, we must do." – Leonardo Da Vinci

Get out of the harbor, house, or hostile environment by tossing all past baggage away, to lighten your load moving forward. Eliminate timewasters.

"Never give up. Today is hard, tomorrow will be worse, but the day after tomorrow

will be sunshine". Jack Ma

During the daily power hour, after coffee, set the intention for the day. Creating good habits creates productivity, makes us feel good (heart), and allows our brain to sense accomplishment. The bonus is the uplifting feel-good endorphins in our head!

The secret code for success, wealth, health, love, and joy comes from within YOU, but you must first unlock the door to possibilities. Go, and grow change your life, which will fuel your success and happiness.

What is your **WHY** and **WHERE**, then create steps between?

"Good fortune is what happens when opportunity meets with planning." Thomas Edison

MY 360°: IF I CAN- YOU CAN!

I discovered a 360° approach when I found myself thrust into running a machine shop. We had a well failure on a farm, so income was needed. Hubby engineered equipment to 100% manufacture a wire mesh conveyor belt for agriculture, instead of assembling parts from suppliers, which created more profit. Then hubby returned to the farm crisis.

Necessity is the mother of invention. I already knew a lot of the customers, but I had to stretch my mechanical aptitude and leadership skills to manage 360° of the business.

New to me was a technical 10,000 sq ft machine shop. I would check on production with the shop manager, hold regular meetings and make lists on whiteboards. But the most productive was walking 360° around to see progress, while stopping to chat with operators to learn needs, challenges, and encourage their efforts as a member of the team. Having timely quality products for customer's, was necessary for sales.

The manufacturing insights helped me as a woman, selling to all male customers in processing plants across all the western states, from border to border.

The question I always asked was, "What can I do to help you today?"

Our products were cost competitive, last longer, and had tighter tolerances. This fueled business growth of 5-fold in 5 years, without borrowing a penny. A lot of effort was needed balancing accounts receivable and payables, plus payroll. Challenging, but richly rewarding when we sold out to a competitor.

>"I alone cannot change the world, but I can cast a stone across the waters to create many ripples." – Mother Teresa

DREAMS TO REALITY

Reflect on Walt Disney's Mickey Mouse and Disneyland project which was rejected over 300 times. His vision seemed foreign, but his passion refused to let him quit, and now there are Disneylands around the world!

As a leader, team up and tame each day with its changes, challenges, and chances.

"Change your thoughts and you change your world."
– Norman Vincent Peale

A successful path involves strategic planning, diligent practice, unwavering perseverance, and the pursuit of obtainment, all infused with the magic of a concrete vision, bottomless desire, and intuition for an accelerated pace. Unfortunately, this cocktail is not on the market, and must be created by you!

Being 125%+ committed to your destination, will inspire the team, and reward the journey.

"Never doubt that a small group of thoughtful committed citizens can change the world; indeed, it's the only thing that ever has." – Margaret Mead

INSIGHTS INTO THE ALASKAIN IDITAROD

Drawing inspiration from the Alaska Iditarod Sled Dog Race, where Mushers lead their teams from behind through treacherous terrains, we uncover the secrets of developing a cohesive team.

"Plan your work for today and every day, then work your plan." Margaret Thatcher

Spanning approximately 1,000 miles of harsh Alaskan terrain, the Iditarod challenges Mushers, and their dog teams. Negotiating frozen waters, mountain passes, and white-out blizzards requires meticulous planning, practice, trust-building, and reliance on relationships. Each dog, vital to the team's success, contributes strength, stamina, and teamwork. Months of rigorous training, preparing alternative routes and stocking supplies are essential.

The course typically runs from Anchorage to Nome, in March for 7-10+ days. Critical decisions, trust, and relationships are paramount for safe passage, with checkpoints serving as rest, health checks and supply stops.

A dog team consists of 12-14 dogs, with a mandatory five online at the finish. Dogs have an innate positive desire to run, each having a critical position for an efficient sled pull.

A coveted golden harness awaits the winning dog, along with cash prizes for the teams.

Mushing is only for the strong-hearted, testing physical and mental abilities to their limits. Navigating the frozen wilderness, conquering fear, and battling unpredictable nature demands maintaining focus, grit, and smart 360° leadership to optimize the team's performance.

Teamwork is essential, as they run together towards unexplored paths. First-time mushers may not reach the top tier, but the challenge propels them to return multiple times before finding the 'winners' circle.

"It is not the strongest of the species that survive, not the most intelligent,

but the one most responsive to change." Charles Darwin

INSIGHTS IN THE 360° DOG TRAINING

The Musher leads teams from behind, after he surveys 360° to expedite success. When leading humans, communication flows to the whole team to gain 'buy in' and wholehearted participation. It takes a team with varied skills and temperaments to create constructive collaboration to stay on the same path, moving forward.

"A leader is one who knows the way, goes the way, and shows the way." John C Maxwell

Much like a Musher carefully selecting a Lead dog for speed, adaptability and strong instincts, leaders should partner with those who desire to share their journey.

1. **FRONT**
2. Observes, socializes, and builds trust with each dog, while aligning their strengths for a synchronized team. Similarly, leaders should explain and work on the plan, investing time in understanding and building trust with team members.
3. **SIDE RIGHT**
4. Standing beside a dog, the Musher trains individual skills, recognizing and rewarding outstanding performances. In leadership, acknowledging and nurturing individual strengths is crucial. Standing alongside creates partnering.
5. **REAR**
6. Transitioning to the rear trusting the teams' instincts, the Musher guides with gentle reins and voiced commands. Similar to a leader educating his team for informed independent decision-making.

7. **SIDE LEFT**

8. Moving to the left The Musher gains a unique perspective to ensure the team is functioning harmoniously. Leaders must adopt various viewpoints to address different team dynamics effectively.

9. **FRONT**

10. Returning to the front again, the Musher praises the team, making mental notes of changes needed. The 360° view offers insights for the Leader while he offers inspiration and best practices.

11. **COMMUNICATION is CRITCAL**

12. Clear and consistent communication, both verbal and non-verbal ensures effective teamwork. A GEE or HAW command (Right or Left) are foreign words to most, but the trained dog team knows the meaning. In leadership, set clear expectations, ensuring they are understood by the team members.

13. **TEAM AND MUSHER CARE DURING THE RACE**

14. The Musher establishes the goals, but on the trail, it is a 360° approach. When the Musher unhooks the team at day's end, before himself, he cares for them, because it is the team that ensures success. All must have food, rest, and warmth.

15. **STRATEGIC POSITIONING**

16. Sled dogs have uncanny senses in the wild. Lead dogs set the pace and direction, swing dogs steer, team dogs offer core strength and wheel dogs stabilize the sled.

Leaders find those with drive and desire to win at their job.

17. **A LEADER CHOOSES THE RIGHT TEMPERAMENT AND SKILLS**

18. Choosing the right temperament and skills for each task ensures optimal team performance.

19. *" It is never too late to be what you might have been."* George Eliot

LESSONS LEARNED

1. The most effective leaders adopt a 360° perspective, rotating their view to gain awareness, insights for improvement, and inspiration for success. This dynamic view enables fine-tuning of strategies and engages/empowers the team to achieve faster success.

2. Succeeding as a Musher/CEO requires steering toward goals, deftly navigating the challenges and maintaining mental focus for success. Sacrifices are made, but quitting is not an option.

3. Leadership requires an unwavering inner drive for high achievement, focus, execution of cleaver plans and commitment with perseverance. Leading teams is worthy, a good endeavor, but is not for all. The team size and what's at stake proportionately increases responsibilities, brain strain from decision making and threat to life balance, especially if things do not go as planned. Some thrive on controlled crisis management. If you cannot take the heat in the kitchen, leave!

4. Let the journey be enjoyable while moving towards your destination, then mentor others. Richness in life is

different for all. While leadership itself may not guarantee financial wealth, it can certainly contribute to a richer and more fulfilling life, both personally and financially. True richness encompasses a holistic concept with various dimensions of intellectual pursuits, well-being, and control of your life.

5. Cultivate wiser version of you, be kind, and your desired impact will flourish, crowning your dreams.

SAY IT, BELIEVE IT AND ACHIEVE IT!

The parallels between winning at life and the mushing experience are evident. Successfully navigating life's unpredictable paths serves as fuel for the mind and soul. Life does not follow straight lines but where there is a will, there is a way.

Climbing metaphorical "Mount Everests" in life doesn't guarantee reaching the pinnacle, and the journey itself involves years of preparation, practice and physical ability with a laser mind set. Not all have the desire to reach the top, therefore a lesser level of attainment is their happy place.

"A clear vision, backed by definite plans, gives you a tremendous feeling of confidence

and personal power." Brian Tracy.

Yes, it is a mind game! Life, like mushing, requires breaking free from doubt, fears, and what ifs. Look only forward through the windshield of life to find joy in doing, not fixating on the rear-view mirror. Release your potential, overcome challenges, and embrace the journey towards your heart's desires. Let's go!

"To handle yourself, use your head; to handle others, use your heart." Eleanor Roosevelt.

Ask yourself: What is my WHY and WHERE? WHY and HOW?

WHAT will be the benefit? WHO will come with me and WHO will be left behind?

Encourage a beneficial vision, while being the leader others can trust, admire, and follow. To make the journey memorable, inject some fun and joy,

MINDSET CHANGE AND PURPOSE

"For I know the plans and thoughts that I have for you,' says the LORD, 'plans for

peace and well-being and not for disaster, to give you a future and a hope" .

Jerimiah 29: 11 amp

Performance increases if all are on the same team with a shared vision, working together. It all starts with planning a strong foundation and moving on the path forward, leaving the past behind, solely focused forward on the future.

Embrace a 360°-degree perspective, adjusting thinking, desires, and habits for lasting success. The 360° degrees approach creates insights, fast-lasting results and land in the winner's circle.

"A man who does not plan long ahead will find trouble at his door." Confucious

Crossroads encompass choices, changes, challenges, compassion, confidence, and celebrating.

A remarkable leader listens to and assesses situations, making insightful decisions for desired outcomes. Leading by example fosters forward progress.

Dreaming of 'what ifs' and acting upon them will help materialize a vision. Illuminate the path to success with your unique vision; the world needs you!

> *"It takes as much energy to wish as it does to plan".* Eleanor Roosevelt.

WHYRUN

A notable example of overcoming the past is the musher, **'WHYRUN.'** He was bullied as a youngster because he had a small stature and ADHD, which kept him continually moving. He was tired of being excluded and not valued. Despite initial skepticism, he emerged as a winner, proving all the naysayers wrong! His WHY was to prove he was smart, fearless, and capable.

YES, BE POSITIVE

Consider as I do, asking God daily for wisdom and direction, to smooth my path, and He multiplied my wins!

By choosing 360° leadership I have made smarter decisions!

You/we are designed uniquely with dreams and passion to become a winner.

For a richer life, practice 360° leadership!

***

To contact Suzanne:

Schedule Lady Suzanne to speak on leadership, team building or fundraising; or engage her personally to arrive at your dream destination.

Schedule a Free 20 minute 'Live your best life' call, you will not regret!

www.Lightning-Leadership.com

Wholeheartedtoday@gmail.com

Rebecca & James Lockwood

Rebecca was born in Saudi Arabia and moved to the US when she was 7. Born to an English mother and a Danish father, you could say she is geographically challenged! James was born in the north of England, traveled the world, and ended up in the US, where he met and married Rebecca.

They live a very unconventional life; Rebecca has a successful coaching practice with over 10,000 hours of business coaching experience. James began his job as CEO/COO/CMO/CFO of Dad Operations after the birth of their second child and has become a coach in their business.

Now, they are living their dreams, including wintering in Colorado with a group of full-time, nomadic families and traveling the world with a home base in Granville, Ohio.

During the COVID-19 pandemic, they embarked on a full-time RV journey across America, visiting 43 National Parks and 32 states. This year, they are set to conquer Everest Base Camp, ticking off just one of the many items on their ambitious bucket list. Sound like high achievers?

Well, they struggled for many years as a married couple - and this is their story. After almost calling it quits, they doubled down and started applying various business, life and marriage coaching tools to their own life. This transformative process led them to develop a unique life operating system they named "Ambitious Living", which has produced amazing results.

Now, they love bringing couples and families closer together, helping them realize their shared vision, and guiding them on how to get traction towards their dreams – with a little less pain than they themselves had once endured.

Our Ambitious Journey
"It was going downhill fast."

By Rebecca & James Lockwood

Life had taken over with two small kids, a business, family commitments, friends, and just everyday chaos. Sure, we still loved each other, and we had a good life from the outside, but our life and marriage didn't feel fulfilling.

Nothing seemed to be working the way we felt it should. We both felt lonely, overwhelmed, and disconnected. We were going down the same river - in 2 different canoes.

We have an unconventional household. (Rebecca runs a successful coaching practice, and James is a stay-at-home dad. Rebecca was growing with big goals and was feeling stuck - she wanted to give up and start over. James wanted to bury his head in the sand. He couldn't dream or look at the future because he was just trying to get through each day.)

We knew there was something better - that we should be in the same canoe, supporting each other, but we just didn't know how. It all felt so overwhelming and intimidating to talk about the stuff that really mattered - and about how far apart we had drifted.

We were:

- Living unfulfilled, knowing there was something better out there.
- Lacking alignment with lots of conflicting priorities.
- Letting problems come between us instead of tackling them together.
- Disconnected from ourselves and each other.

- Overwhelmed and managing marriage, kids, a business, and life poorly.

We knew we had to do something…so we started our Ambitious Journey - applying various business, life and marriage coaching tools to their own life. We tried a lot of things, A LOT, until we finally figured it out. Are we perfect? No. Do we have it all figured out all the time? No. It wasn't all smooth or easy. There were tears, tension and pain.

However, today, we're now more in love, more connected, and living with more intention than ever before. We love sharing what we've learned with other couples who want to:

- Align on their Vision
- Cultivate the right Mindset
- Connect more deeply
- Get results through Action

That's how we came up with the Ambitious Model, and here's what we've gained from our Ambitious Journey so far. We have:

- A stronger connection with each other at an extremely deep and intimate level
- Solved problems faster with mutually beneficial solutions
- Achieved dreams which were previously mere conversations
- Made significant progress on our way towards our long-term big goal and bucket list items
- A plan we work on weekly, monthly, and annually
- Fixed, and more importantly, aligned goals

- Deep, meaningful rituals
- Control and freedom
- Fun, laughter, contentment, and peace (relative lol)

In essence, we created a model or framework that lets us control our future.

> *"The best way to predict the future is to create it."*
> *- Peter Drucker*

Let's start with why a model or framework is crucial for couples (if this already sounds horrible, just give us blind faith for a few more paragraphs).

Every couple has one whether they know it or not. It is how they set priorities, divide tasks, parent, use resources, dream, set goals, support each other, solve problems, approach the world, view their mind, body, and soul, communicate, and connect.

However, most couples never think about their relationship or life through this lens (we certainly didn't, too, at first). This results in mediocrity - just floating through life, or worse, chaos, frustration, and/or divorce. Ultimately, without a deliberate model, they never realize their full potential as individuals, a couple, or as a family.

In fact, the US has a 50%+ divorce rate. Imagine the marriages that could have been saved if these couples had a model to connect, communicate, set goals, resolve issues - and stay in the same canoe.

This is why a model is important. You may be thinking, "This sounds like it will kill all spontaneity and romance. This doesn't sound fun at all." And you'd be dead wrong.

> *"If you want better results, you need a better system."*
> *- W. Edwards Deming*

In truth, a couple using a model will realize more of their dreams and ambitions, be happier, have more fun, live longer, embrace spontaneity, nurture heightened romance and intimacy, overcome life's challenges through mutual support, and connect at an extremely intimate level.

They develop a "we/us" approach to everything, embodying the couple that remains in love after 60 years, having accomplished a majority of their goals and dreams.

If that sounds like something you want, here are a few more things we discovered on our Ambitious Journey:

- This is not therapy
- This is not rigid
- This is not prescriptive

You can take the tools, concepts and activities as suggestions and customize them to make them yours. We certainly did. We took proven business, life, and marriage coaching tools, combined them with ancient wisdom, and adapted them to our life and relationship. We're just letting you know what worked for us and what you can gain from using it.

So now that you know why a model is important and what it can do for you, it is important to understand how it works.

We discovered that every successful couple is rock solid in 4 critical elements: Vision, Mindset, Connect, and Action. Like a jigsaw puzzle, the model incorporates these essential elements as pieces. Just as a puzzle remains unfinished without each piece, your relationship's picture remains incomplete without these critical elements.

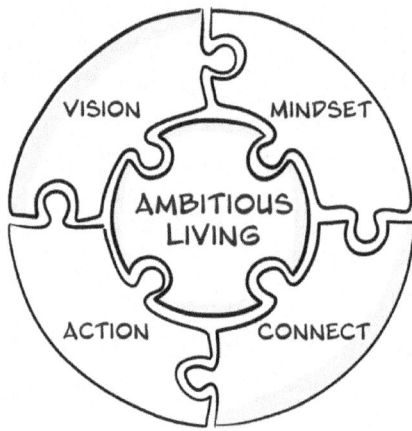

We'll give you a high-level view of why each is critical and how to strengthen each element.

THE VISION ELEMENT

Have you ever agreed on long-term plans only to find out later that you really didn't? Have you ever talked about dreams that never materialized? If so, you're not alone. This is a common challenge faced by many couples.

James wanted a house with a white picket fence. Rebecca wanted to be a nomad, RVing around America. "We kept going in circles, which turned into arguments pushing us further apart," said Rebecca. "It was very frustrating."

A misaligned vision is a common problem caused by a lack of clarity, alignment, agreement, and documentation. You might have similar goals but different ideas on how to reach them. Or, you might have goals that seem conflicting. How can you possibly both get what you want? You have talked about dreams but have different priorities. You've talked about plans for the next month, but things keep getting in the way.

Now imagine yourselves with a written vision of your future. You've figured out how both of you can achieve your individual and joint goals – together. You've agreed on it.

You've prioritized it. You've written it down. You've decided how you'll work on it together. Everything is in sync. When life gets in the way, you're able to stay focused and work through it together.

"Now," continued Rebecca, "we have an aligned plan with steps, priorities, and a budget. Even better, we've stopped the endless arguments and discussions and are making real progress.

"When we boiled it down, we realized we could have both - we didn't have to compromise. It was extremely freeing, and the problems stopped coming between us, and became problems to solve together - they were even kind of fun to solve."

This is what being 100% in the Vision Element does for you. You'll both be working together towards the same long-term and short-term goals. There will be less frustration and fewer arguments. More will get done in less time. You'll be able to say no to things that don't align with your vision.

The tool we developed to strengthen our Vision Element is called the Ambitious Vision Plan, or "AVP". It helps you get aligned around the answers to 9 simple questions:

1. What are your Values?
2. What is your Why?
3. What is your Big Goal?
4. What is on your Bucket List?
5. What are your Rituals?
6. What is your 3-Year Vision?
7. What are your 1-Year Goals?
8. What are your 90-Day Rocks?
9. What is your 1 Commitment to me?

Once you are aligned, and these 9 questions are answered, you'll be on your way to being 100% rock solid in the Vision Element.

THE MINDSET ELEMENT

Do you know anyone who thinks nothing is possible? Perhaps someone with a victim mentality, always blaming others for every setback, or someone who finds problems in everything and then points fingers? Do you know anyone who gives up when they only have 1% to go to finish?

Imagine what a relationship would look like if such thinking prevailed. Surprisingly, many relationships suffer from this exact issue, and it stems from an unhealthy mindset.

In such an environment, limitations would be placed on everything. Nothing would be possible. Joy and celebration would be non-existent. Arguments would be endless. Dreams, goals, forward movement, and a deep, wonderful connection would be impossible.

Your mindset determines how you handle challenges, plan, achieve dreams, build a deep, lasting relationship, laugh, celebrate, support each other no matter what, and feel intimately connected.

Imagine if Nelson Mandela had given up after 27 years in prison or if Beethoven had stopped composing because he was going deaf. Consider Marie Curie, Stephen Hawking, and even yourself?

These individuals are all examples of resilience - they did not let their circumstances shape their thinking. Instead, they used their mindset to shape their circumstances. You can do the same with a strong, healthy mindset.

"What if life was not happening to you, it was happening for you."

Tony Robbins

Imagine a relationship where anything is possible. Where there is a mutually beneficial solution to every challenge. Where support is unconditional. Where even arguments are viewed as positive events. Where you both feel intimately in sync. Where every goal and dream is met. This is what 100% in the Mindset Element looks like. "We're not there yet, but this is our goal," indicated James.

THE CONNECT ELEMENT

Do you ever feel lonely or disconnected from your partner? Maybe sometimes you feel misunderstood. At times, you might even wonder why you and your partner are arguing. Do you feel like us - on the same river but in 2 different canoes? Perhaps not even on the same river?

If so, the problem is a lack of Connection. You know when your connection is off, but it is hard to put your finger on exactly why.

Connecting often feels effortless in the early stages of a relationship—during the dating phase and the initial years of marriage. You feel that incredible energy between you that comes from shared positive emotional experiences. However, that energy, trust and vulnerability that was driving you towards an ongoing intimate level of connection is just not there anymore.

"I always longed for a deep, meaningful connection but didn't know how to ask for it," stated Rebecca. "James felt like he was in an interrogation room when I approached it. It made him shut down."

A poor connection is caused by a lack of practice, understanding and intentionality. Connection with your partner is like a plant, and like any plant, it needs to be watered, fed and get enough sunlight. The Connect Element is about understanding the balance of water, food, and sunlight - and then nurturing it.

Imagine not feeling like roommates but like soul mates. You both feel seen and heard. You feel aligned. You have date nights and rituals that keep you connected. You spend quality time (not just a lot of time) together. You can actually talk about your level of connection.

You share an unequaled level of trust and vulnerability. You can talk about and tell each other everything and anything. You approach the world as "we". You become the couple that people look at and say, "Look at them. They are truly connected." That is 100% in the Connect Element.

THE ACTION ELEMENT

"Action is the most important key to any success."

-Tony Robbins

By now, you've probably thought of a few things you want to do - but have no idea how to get it all done. You have a vision around which you are aligned. You are approaching life with the right mindset. You are deepening and strengthening your connection. But what do you do to make it a reality? To make it stick?

"We were putting our vision on paper, going to seminars, learning about ourselves but when we'd get back home, life got busy and we just reverted to the way it used to be," said James.

"It was frustrating. We tried but we just didn't know how to keep it going. We didn't know how to create action or lasting habits from all we had learned. I also made the mistake of committing to too much or to the wrong things."

Imagine a couple with the best of intentions but struggling to follow through. They schedule date nights, but they rarely happen. Time is double booked with different friends. They feel like an Uber service.

Agreed-upon projects start (sometimes) but never reach completion - they both think the other person is going to do the next step. Activities aren't assigned, agreed upon or led by the person who is best at doing them. They don't know who's doing what. Things get out of whack when kids, work, friends, etc. get thrown in the mix.

This is caused by a lack of focus, accountability, clarity, and prioritization. These symptoms are the direct result of a lack of a systematic approach to getting things done: weekly, monthly, quarterly and annually.

Now, picture a couple where 90% of date nights actually happen, weekly to-dos are checked off, progress towards their vision is crystal clear, they prioritize and adjust as needed, they have fun, and they celebrate their success. They are in control and living their best life every day, week, month, and year.

This is what 100% in the Action Element looks, sounds, and feels like. You have a cadence and rhythm to life. You are accomplishing the things on your Ambitious Vision Plan (bucket list items, dreams, goals, etc.). You are making your future happen.

SUMMARY

So now you know how it all started for us, why a model is important, how each element of the model can help you, and what you look like when each element is 100% rock solid.

You and your partner will be aligned on your vision, approaching life with a strong, healthy mindset, connecting more deeply and getting results through action.

Here is a simple summary of the Ambitious Model and the tools we found useful. While we couldn't describe most of them here, you can get many of them for free on our website.

Core Element	What's it all about	Tools & Approaches We Used
Vision	Aligning on, agreeing on, and documenting your vision and plan.	Ambitious Vision Plan (AVP), Align at the Top.
Mindset	Cultivating and approaching life and your relationship with a strong, healthy mindset.	Growth Checkup, Abundance Checkup, Be…Do…Have, Progress not Perfection.
Connect	Connecting more deeply with intentionality and by strengthening your connect muscle.	Connection Assessment, Bank Account, Kolbe A to A™, 5 Connection Levels.
Action	Getting results through focus, clarity, prioritization, accountability, and a systematic approach.	3 Qs (The 3 Couple's Questions), Weekly Sync, Scorecard, Pink/Blue Chart.

And so, that's how our story unfolds. When we started this, it felt clunky and awkward. Over the past six years, we experimented, made adjustments, and refined our approach to find what worked best for us.

We asked our coach, Tom Bouwer, to help us simplify, create and translate our learnings into a model that could be shared with others. (FYI - Tom has published 3 books, including "What the Heck is EOS?" with Gino Wickman, and has sold over 1 million copies). This became the Ambitious Model, Ambitious Journey, and Ambitious Living.

As we began sharing Ambitious Living with other couples, we discovered that everyone needs to find their own nuances and make tweaks to tailor it to their unique Ambitious Journey. What we also found is that the model and tools can work for everyone—provided they want them to.

Now, we make our decisions based on our core values and goals. Our Ambitious Vision Plan is like having a GPS system for our life. When traffic hits, it helps us navigate challenges and keeps us on the right path.

We recently invested time in mapping out our year, and what made it even cooler was having the kids actively participate in decision-making and goal setting. How amazing is that?

Our life and marriage are more than fulfilling. Things, most days, seem to be working the way we want them to work. We feel together, connected, and less overwhelmed. We're in the same canoe, paddling in the same direction, supporting each other, and loving every moment of it (well, we do all have our days).

***

To contact Rebecca and James:

www.ambitious-couples.com

www.ambitious-living.com

info@ambitious-living.com

Or feel free to contact us directly:

james@be-moor.com 214-336-3663

rebecca@be-moor.com 214-830-5003

Afterword

Life and business are always a series of transitions... people, places, and things that shape who we are as individuals. Often, you never know that the next catalyst for improving your business and life is around the corner, in the next person you meet, next mentor you hire or the next book you read.

Jim Britt has spent over four decades influencing individuals and entrepreneurs with strategies to grow their business, developing the right mindset and mental toughness to thrive in today's business environment and to live a better life overall.

Allow all you have read in this book to create a new you, to reinvent yourself and your business model if required, because every business and life level requires a different you. It is your journey to craft.

Cracking the Rich Code is a series that offers much more than a book. It is a community of like-minded influencers from around the world. A global movement. Each chapter is like opening a surprise gift, that just may contain the one idea that changes everything for you. Watch for future releases and add them to your collection.

The work of Jim Britt has filled seminar rooms to maximum capacity and created a worldwide demand. If you get the opportunity to attend one of his live events, jump at the chance. You'll be glad you did.

Become a coauthor: If you are a coach, speaker, consultant of entrepreneur and would like to get the details about becoming a coauthor in the next Cracking the Rich Code book in the series, contact Jim britt at: support@jimbritt.com

STRUGGLING WITH MONEY ISSUES?

Check out Jim's latest program "Cracking the Rich Code" which focuses on the subconscious programs influencing one's financial success, that keeps most living a life of mediocrity. This powerful four-month program is designed to change one's relationship with money and reset your money programming to that of the wealthy. More details at: www.CrackingTheRichCode.com

To Schedule Jim Britt as a featured speaker at your next convention or special event, online or live, email: support@jimbritt.com

Master each moment as they become hours that become days.

Make it a great life!

Your legacy awaits.

STAY IN TOUCH

www.JimBritt.com

www.poweroflettinggo.com

www.CrackingTheRichCode.com

www.ingramcontent.com/pod-product-compliance
Lightning Source LLC
LaVergne TN
LVHW021801060526
838201LV00058B/3195